Stump City

Stump City

Mike Quigley

2007

Stump City

INTRODUCTION

My father nears death, and memories are coming back that I've either forgotten or tried to forget. Dad's closeness to meeting his Maker has given me the incentive to retell my youth in the forties and fifties.

It was a time when Mom stayed home to take care of the "Wee Ones" and tried to make ends meet on what Dad took home from his full and part time jobs. It was a time of second-hand clothes, lots of potatoes, turkey necks, outdoor plumbing, once-a-week baths, and hard cider in the basement.

In many respects, it was a wonderful time. In a few, it was a terrible time.

This is a story that is mostly fact sprinkled with a tad of exaggeration for seasoning. The latter has to be forgiven because the Irish blood that courses though my veins has always affected my memory.

The brood consists of seven children—four girls and three boys. We are all about two years apart. A Catholic priest would call it perfect placement and a fine example for Church growth. Their names will come into play a bit later as each arrives on the scene.

Since I am the oldest, it is easier for me to show the ballooning of the family from a first-hand perspective.

Before I get started, I would like to tell you about the physical layout of Stump City at the time the events in the story took place.

Stump City is in Central New York State a few miles north of the village of Skaneateles. It is across Skaneateles Creek from the main part of Skaneateles Falls behind the Welch Allyn Company and is considered a "suburb" of Skaneateles Falls.

The main street in Skaneateles Falls is Jordan Road. The Skaneateles Short Line Railroad runs close to Jordan Road from Skaneateles to Hartlot where it connects to the Auburn Railroad. The Short Line is considered the shortest privately owned railroad in the country.

Stump Road intersects Jordan Road right by Rodak's Bar and the Welch Allyn Company. It runs west down a hill and across Skaneateles Creek and back up the hill as it goes through Stump City. Stump Road ends in the town of Sennett some four miles away. The road is lined with sugar maples and stone fences on both sides once it crosses County Line Road and leaves Stump City.

Stump City has eleven homes on Stump Road with plenty of overhanging sugar maples on both sides.

Phillips Road runs off Stump Road at the top of the hill coming up from the creek, goes up a slight hill to the south and then takes a right-hand turn heading west to County Line Road. There are only four houses on Phillips Road.

The road we live on is a dead end street with no name and is right behind Welch Allyn. It starts at the same point on Stump Road that Phillips Road does and runs north parallel to Skaneateles Creek. There is a narrow wood between the creek and the road with no houses on that side. Six houses are on the west side of the road. John and Helen McEneny owned the first house, and we lived in the second one.

The total population of Skaneateles Falls is around three hundred with about seventy living in Stump City.

Many of the people in the community are of Irish descent, which explains the four thriving drinking holes either in or close to Skaneateles Falls.

Most of the men are employed by the four factories either in or close to Skaneateles Falls.

That should be enough to give you mental picture of the area. If it's not, take a look at the little map.

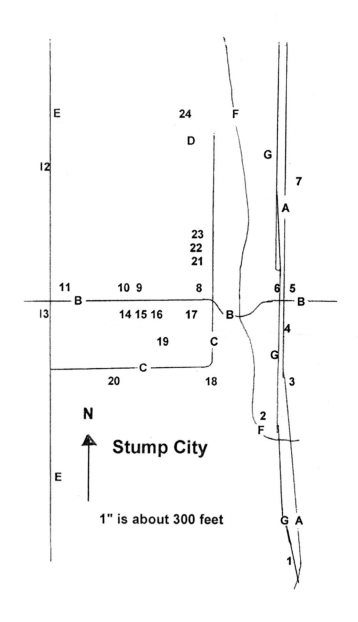

Stump City

N

1" is about 300 feet

KEY

1. Cronaeur's Store
2. Waterbury Felt Co.
3. Skaneateles Falls School
4. St. Bridget's Church
5. Rodaks Bar
6. Welch Allyn
7. Tambroni
8. Wickham
9. Cashin
10. Quigley Grandparents
11. Walters
12. O'Hara
13. Fiddler Bin
14. Scott/Calnon
15. Big Jim McEneny
16. Dad's birthplace
17. Waltons
18. Phillips
19. Mooney
20. Sheridan
21. John/Helen McEneny
22. Our House
23. Moore
24. Kimak
A. Jordan Road
B. Stump Road
C. Phillips Road
D. Our Street
E. County Line Road
F. Skaneateles Creek
G. Short Line RR

MOM AND DAD

I'm the finished product of a full-blooded Englishwoman and a full-blooded second generation Irishman. There's a conflict here that will play a part in what is written on later pages.

My mother (Ethel Simpson) and my father (John V., or "Vince", Quigley) met because of Hitler and the Japanese. Dad was in the United States Army and Mom was in the English Land Army. The Army is a familiar term to you, but Land Army might not ring a bell. Most members of the Land Army were females. The girls worked on farms and filled other positions left vacant by men who had entered the military. I suppose they were the first "Rosie the Riveters".

Mom worked on a farm tending the cattle, getting in crops, and doing other jobs necessary to feed the British war machine. It was a hard life, but she was a willing worker.

From what I can gather, she liked it for the most part. Maybe she just blocked out the bad and remembered the good when she told me about it in later times.

Dad was based near a military hospital close to Mom's hometown of Ellesmere. As a youngster he never told me much about what he did. At a much later time, he reluctantly mentioned interrogating prisoners at a prisoner of war camp near Ellesmere and going off on missions to North Africa dressed in civilian clothing.

My parents met at a Saturday night dance in the Ellesmere Town Hall and romance bloomed. I think Mom was out to find a man because the R.A.F. pilot who had been dating her, and who was also billeted in her parents' home, ditched her. He was shot down and wounded and ended up falling in love with one of the nurses who was taking care of him. When she found out about the pilot's new love, Mom sold all of the clothes he had left in the house on the black market and bought herself a new wardrobe. Was Dad the rebound man?

They were married in January of 1945.

Within only a few months after they were married, the Germans surrendered and Dad had to get prepared to go fight the Japanese. The only thing that saved him, and many thousands more, were the "big bombs" dropped on two Japanese cities. After V.J. Day, Dad had to wait until November of 1945 to be shipped home on the *U.S.S. Saratoga*, an aircraft carrier. He became a civilian again on December 7th. It's fitting because that day is what made him run to the Army recruiter four years earlier.

Before he came home from England, Dad wrote a letter to John McEneny, who was like a second father to Dad and also lived in Stump City. He asked John to not sell the house next door to his own home until he could look it over.

Mr. McEneny wrote back to Dad and told him that he would wait and not put the house on the market until Dad got back. When he did get home, Dad looked over the place, Mr. McEneny set a price, and Dad shook his hand. The deal was closed.

Mrs. McEneny, along with her daughter Rose, Dad, his sisters and brother fixed up the interior with new wallpaper and paint. They all worked hard, long hours to make the place fit to live in.

As I said earlier, our house is located on a nameless street in Stump City. I don't ever remember seeing another street in Stump City without a name, unless some car had knocked down a street sign or a prankster had stolen it.

Before the war, Dad had worked for Mr. Cronaeur in his general store in Skaneateles Falls. He came back from war to his same position as store clerk until he could find a better paying job.

It didn't take Dad long to find one. He started working in Camillus Cutlery where many types of knives are made.

Michael

I got the impression that I was conceived as part of the big V.E. celebration—something on the same order of a baby explosion after a natural disaster or the power going out for a long spell. The time sequence seems to work out rather well. I was born in Ellesmere, England, on February 9th of 1946—the first year of what was to be called the Baby Boom Generation—and spent the first fourteen months of my life on foreign soil. Do I remember anything of that time? Nope.

Mom told me many times that I cried a great deal. My crying must have bothered her terribly for her to bring it up so often. Out of desperation from my continual wailing, she took me to an Army doctor. He said that I was malnourished and put me on evaporated milk. Mom was overworked caring for her ailing mother and me and underfed because there was a food shortage in England. Thus, her milk supply was a bit skimpy.

Every time I cried she stuck a bottle filled with the evaporated milk into my mouth. That probably explains why I weighed thirty pounds at six months and was too fat to walk until I was much older than one. To this day, I can't stand the smell of the stuff.

I didn't find out until recently that England didn't get back on its feet until 1960 and that food and other necessaries were

3

rationed until then. Maybe that explains a very serious change in the life of our family a few years later. I'll tell you more about it on future pages.

In March of 1947, Mom, with her few belongings jammed into two suitcases, and I boarded a chartered Merchant Marine vessel bound for New York City. It was packed with hundreds of other war brides and their babies.

Some of the women didn't understand that they were going to be in America for a long time and left their babies with relatives. By the time they figured out what was really happening, it was too late. It took many months for the babies to catch up to their mothers. In some cases, the babies were never reunited with their moms.

On board the ship, Mom kept me all bundled up and in a dresser drawer she had wedged open so that it wouldn't fall out. She said that it was a very rough crossing and many women, including her, got seasick. It turned out to be one of the worst winters on record for storms in the North Atlantic.

One woman caused a minor panic during a bad storm. She yelled, "Grab your lifejackets and babies, girls. We're going down!"

It took the stewards some time to calm the mothers, and the mothers a longer time still to get their babies settled back down.

I can't imagine a shipload of crying babies.

I was probably one of the loudest.

Dad and Uncle Jimmy traveled by train from Syracuse to New York City to meet us. I have a vague memory of someone telling me that they both got drunk the night before they met us at the pier. It could have been Mom who told me this. I also was told that Dad thought it was one of the greatest moments of his life when he saw me for the first time.

Was one of them a sign of things to come?

Mom had to stand in line for a long while to get processed through immigration. She had to sign all kinds of papers and hold my tremendous weight at the same time. If I was thirty pounds at six months, who knows what I weighed in at when I was past one.

When she finally saw Dad, she said, "Here, you take him."

I immediately changed hands.

I am not sure if it was because Mom's arms were too weary to hold me much longer, and she was afraid she'd drop me or if she was tired of having to take care of me for over a year all by herself.

It took Mom a long time to get somewhat over being home-sick. It was very hard for her to adjust to her new life in this country, especially in Stump City—Dad's Irish family was all living there.

Grandma and Grandpa Quigley

Grandpa and Grandma Quigley had both arrived from the "Old Country" in the early 1900's. Until they died they were very Irish in their talk and mannerisms. Grandpa's first job in America was working on the Auburn Railroad Line repairing track, grades, and bridges.

Before she met and married Grandpa, Grandma got a job as a seamstress for Helen Hayes (the actress) in New York City. I know she didn't have well-connected friends, so I don't know how she got the position.

I don't think either one of them liked the idea of Dad marrying an Englishwoman. Plus, there were the McEneny, Sheridan, Phillips, Cashin, Major, O'Hara, Keegan, and Moore families to add fuel to the fire of how the English had slaughtered and starved the Irish over many centuries of occupation.

It was tough for Mom to be accepted into the community. I think that some of the Irish who lived there focused their hatred of the English onto her.

She must have had old relatives who had the power to control an entire population for the neighbors to treat her so badly.

Grandpa Quigley didn't talk to me very much when I was little. He did let me follow him around the house if I stayed out of his way.

I remember being in his house and watching him shave. I was awestruck by the straight razor that he sharpened on the leather strop. The shaving cream on his face looked just like whipped cream. I always wanted to taste it to see if it went down as well as the cream, but never got up the nerve to ask.

I'm sure Grandpa would have let me give it a go and then smiled when a frown appeared on my face.

During the proper season, Grandpa, in his Sunday best replete with suspenders, made it a ritual to come down to our house after Sunday Mass at St. Bridget's to have a "wee" glass of hard cider. Dad kept a quarter keg of the stuff in the musty cellar. It was enough off the dirt floor to show respect and reverence for the brew. The season was short because the cider would turn after being in the barrel awhile. Dad and Grandpa made sure that it never got a chance to turn.

Grandpa wouldn't be around much once the cider was gone, but he would start up his weekly visits to the cellar once the season came again.

Tess, Grandma Quigley, was hit by a stroke when Dad was defending the country. She was only in her early fifties when it happened. Her left arm hung limply by her side, and her left leg didn't work very well. When she sat down, she'd have to lift the bad arm with her good one to place it on her lap.

Her eyes held a mix of emotions: a mix of love, frustration, and anger. Her anger would leave her eyes and enter her mouth and body when she didn't like what one of her children said or did. Her frustration would show when she was being fed. Her love would show when she saw me walk into the house.

Grandma was a vibrant lion caged in a wicker wheelchair.

I remember her talking to Aunt Mary (Dad's oldest sister) in garbled words. Aunt Mary understood, but I sure didn't. One time something struck her funny while Aunt Mary was feeding her with a spoon, and Grandma began to laugh uncontrollably. She was eating oatmeal at the time, and it was coming out of the edges of her mouth and landing on her bib. I was amazed at both actions because I thought only babies let this happen while eating, and I'd never seen Grandma laugh so deeply before. She had tears running down her face.

I don't remember her laughing again after that, but she did try to smile on occasion.

Grandma could walk a little, but it was a mighty chore for her. Someone had to be at her side. She had to think ahead about using the toilet because it took so long for her to get up out of her wheelchair and get herself situated in the bathroom.

She had a high-backed wicker wheelchair that she sat in most of the day. Her little frame seemed to be consumed by the big-wheeled contraption. I hated the thing because it always looked like it was trying to hold her down. Any slight move made the wicker make crackling noises in protest.

When the weather was decent, Aunt Mary would wrap a blanket around Grandma's legs, put a shawl around her shoulders, and wheel her out onto the porch where she would stay for long periods of time watching neighborhood activities with great interest. She got to see Mr. Scott, who lived across the street, a lot because he spent so much time tending to his flower gardens. She wasn't out there at all during the winter, but I know she enjoyed being on the porch when she had the chance.

I don't think she ever left Stump City after her stroke. She couldn't even get to church because there were too many steps.

I was a little afraid of Grandma because of a story I had heard. She was just a bit of a thing but suffered no shenanigans from Grandpa. When he came home late on payday because he was attending "sacred services" at Murray's Bar with his working buddies, she would make the poor man feel pretty small. I don't think she was beneath giving him a good, solid punch when he was in The Condition, but the tongue-lashings were what really seemed to hurt him.

I'd settle for a tongue lashing, if I could only hear her real voice.

Grandpa wasn't that tall, but he made Grandma look like a midget. When he spoke to me it was in a soft but firm voice. His large belly was made to look even bigger because he always had suspenders on to hold up his pants. The straps curved out from his chest, over his belly, and disappeared at his belt line. His hands weren't that big. They were clean but looked dirty because of all the calluses, cuts, and scabs they suffered from working the machinery at Waterbury Felt Company. He walked in a slow, steady, determined way with his eyes focused on going forward and not glancing back.

The only time Grandpa would look back was after he had a drink or two.

Sometimes, when the train whistle on the roof of Waterbury Felt Company blew to signal the men and women it was time to quit for the day, I'd be at his house sitting on the porch with Grandma. We'd both watch him come up Stump Road with his black metal lunch box hanging from his side. He would be walking the same way he always did, except his pace would be a tad slower. His pants would be down some from their normal resting spot because the suspenders would have lost some of their control over his always over-sized dark blue pants during the course of the day.

Grandpa always walked to and from work. It was only a five-minute walk in good weather. He never owned a car nor did he learn to drive.

He didn't say much to either Grandma or me when he got onto the porch. He'd lean over and kiss Grandma on the forehead, go into the house, wash his hands and face in the kitchen sink, and head to his over-stuffed chair in the living room after turning on the big wooden radio.

No one bothered him for a good while. He needed time to rest before supper.

Grandpa worked at Waterbury Felt Company for many years operating and maintaining the huge machines. Wool blankets of different sizes, shapes, and colors were made there and shipped all over the world.

I remember walking by the factory when I was old enough to go to Cronaeur's General Store for Mom or Big Jim McEneny and seeing Grandpa working. Once in a while he would be leaning out the window by his work area to get a breath of fresh air, and he'd give me a wave and a smile as I walked by. I still remember the sound of the wooden shuttle-cocks going back and forth and the sharp bang they'd make at each end of the huge looms. The speed of the things was quite amazing to a boy of my age.

Dad in His Youth

Dad was a hard worker as a boy. When he was old enough, he took over the milking of the little Guernsey cow in the barn behind the house before and after school. He tended to the lay-ing hens, slopped the pigs kept in a pen behind the barn, and helped Grandpa work the big garden until his brother Jimmy was old enough to give him a hand.

When he was a young teenager, he'd work summers and after school at Ross Caddy's big dairy farm a mile or so away. He'd be there before the sun came up to help milk and feed the hundred or so Holstein cows. There was no electricity, so the milking had to be done by hand. The hours were very long when crops had to be planted or harvested. Dad wouldn't get home until the afternoon milking was done and the sun had set.

When the weather was good, Mr. Caddy would often say to Dad, "Vinnie, we have got to make hay while the sun is shining."

Dad had an adventurous spirit. One time he and a few friends borrowed a canoe and were paddling around during the spring thaw in the mill pond behind a factory. They got too daring and ended up going over the twelve-foot falls. Some friends pulled them out.

It was big news and the story with a picture was printed in the newspaper in Syracuse.

When he graduated from eighth grade at the Skaneateles Falls School, Dad went to high school in Skaneateles. He did well in school, acted in school plays, and boxed for the school team.

There wasn't much to Dad as far as size goes, but he was tough as nails. Hard work did that to him. He was of average height and only weighed around one twenty-five after a good meal.

When war was declared in 1941, Dad enlisted in the Army for the duration.

After boot camp he went through more training at Fort Dix while he waited for orders to go overseas. He boxed on his regimental team to keep in shape.

With time to kill, some officers decided to have a boxing match between Dad's regiment and another one. Dad was picked to fight the heavyweight champion of the other regiment.

The day of the fight was set. Given the size difference, Dad was a heavy underdog. The betting odds were very one-sided.

Dad knocked the much bigger man out in the first round. Those who knew something about boxing, and had seen Dad box, won small fortunes.

Not long after the fight, Dad and thousands of other soldiers boarded transport ships headed for England.

The Quigley Aunts and Uncles

Dad had three sisters and one brother. All were still living with Grandma and Grandpa when he returned to Stump City. It must have been tight quarters because it was a small, three-bedroom home.

Aunt Mary

Aunt Mary was the oldest. She was a very stern, thin, serious woman who enjoyed controlling the daily happenings in other people's lives. Even after she got married to Uncle Bob and worked at International Harvester as a secretary, she'd be in control of her house and Grandma's when she got back from work.

She'd run back and forth in Grandma's kitchen and gave off an air of divine purpose. She made her movements and actions appear to be more important than what anyone else could possibly be doing around her. Her hands would flash from the cupboard to the sink top or the table with amazing quickness. Everyone gave her a wide berth when she was on a mission.

She was always on a mission.

I kept out of her way, especially when she ran the loud Hoover vacuum cleaner with the red light on the front. The machine looked like a one-eyed monster. She'd be so intent on what she was doing, I'm sure I would have been sucked into the bag without her even noticing.

Shortly after Dad came home from the war, Uncle Bob and Aunt Mary got married and set up house in a small trailer on the narrow lot next to my grandparents' house.

I remember the trailer being a silver color with a rounded top like an Air Streamer. It looked small to me then.

That's saying something because most things looked big and distances seemed greater then than they do now.

Uncle Bob was considered to be a member of the Quigley family. He was a short, slight, frail man with a very tender way about him.

Uncle Bob tried to join the Army, but he couldn't pass the physical.

He and Dad grew up together and were the best of friends.

Aunt Pat

A year or so after Dad was born, Aunt Pat entered the world. I remember her with a warm feeling. She was a beautiful woman blessed with a loving smile, striking hair, and bright eyes.

She stayed out of Aunt Mary's way too. She did so in a very casual manner and without any fear. It was an art she had learned over many years, and Aunt Mary never showed a look or gave an impression toward Aunt Pat that she was invading her conquered territory in a takeover mission.

Aunt Pat was the only one to get a college education. She became a teacher.

Going away to college was an excellent way to get away from Aunt Mary. Aunt Pat was very smart and probably figured out this means of escape at a young age.

She married Danny Calnon, when I was still very young, and fled to Rochester.

Seventy miles was a considerable traveling distance without an interstate highway, and Aunt Mary never traveled much.

I missed her because she was very nice to me and had a calming affect on Aunt Mary.

Aunt Ann

Aunt Ann was the fourth child. She was a tiny woman who had a slight stutter when she got excited. She was very small when she was born and never grew much.

As a baby, Grandma would put Aunt Ann in a shoebox and place her in the kitchen stove under low heat with the oven door open.

When I heard about this, I gained a new respect for her. I figured she must be very tough to survive being baked slowly in an oven. I'd sneak looks at any areas of skin on her not covered with clothes for burn marks. I never found any.

There's something in the Holy Book about a bunch of guys entering a big oven and coming out fine. Aunt Ann did okay too.

When she grew up, Aunt Ann walked a bit bent over, as if the weight of the world was on her shoulders. Maybe it was the weight of Aunt Mary on her back or her way of moving around so that Aunt Mary would have a harder time seeing her.

She'd do whatever Aunt Mary asked and as quickly as she could. Aunt Mary expected her commands to be obeyed at once and as fast as humanly possible. Aunt Ann tried her darnedest but never came up to Aunt Mary's standards—poor woman.

Her laugh still rings in my ears. It was a good, honest laugh coming from her heart. She was happy most of the time, especially when Aunt Mary was working or at the trailer. The house would be calmer. Her stutter seemed to lessen and her back seemed to straighten more as the time passed that Aunt Mary was away from the house.

Uncle Jimmy

My Uncle Jimmy was the last one to join the crew. He was a wild man for that time period. He actually had a "woody" station wagon. It was the best car around. He liked to hunt, drink, ski, raise roosters, and go out with lots of different girls.

He was a tall, thin man with dark, thick, well-attended hair. His voice was wonderful to listen to when he struck up a song, usually an Irish ballad.

He would often come home late. I'm sure Aunt Mary noted the time. She'd give him what-for the next morning when he finally dragged himself out of bed.

It must have hurt his head to have her yelling at him because he'd have a hard time keeping it in a normal position until later in the day when he'd become his usual, laughing self again.

Uncle Jimmy was good to me. He'd even let me help feed the roosters, his most valued possessions at the time. They were kept in separate cages in the little barn out back. The roosters didn't seem to like each other, and Jimmy told me to keep my fingers away from the cages. They scared me some, but I was anxious to please him. I tried not to show my fear of them when he was around.

It took me several years to figure out why Uncle Jimmy raised them. After all, what use are roosters if they don't lay eggs.

He would take me for rides in his wonderful car to Skaneateles or Auburn to run errands for Aunt Mary. As he drove he'd tell me crazy stories as he puffed on one cigarette after another.

Dad said that Uncle Jimmy had "the gift of gab."

Uncle Jimmy liked to run lots of errands just to get out of the house.

It was a grand way to get out of Grandma's house when I was left there while Mom and Dad went shopping and didn't want me to go with them.

All of the children in the Quigley clan attended Skaneateles Falls School. It was over the creek and the railroad tracks. The school was only a few minutes from their house and close to St. Bridget's Church.

I never got any stories about how hard it was to walk to school because even I could understand that distance.

Both Jimmy and Ann didn't complete high school. One didn't because he had better things to do. The other didn't because she didn't have the mental power to get all the way through.

At that time an eighth grade education was pretty good. Some of the kids stopped right there and got jobs. They even got an eighth grade diploma.

Uncle Jimmy eventually did get his high school diploma by going to night school in Auburn.

He must have really wanted to graduate because nights were made for him.

Terry

Less than a year after Mom and I got settled into living in Stump City, my sister, Mary Teresa, was born. My life as the sole attention-getter was over. I was no longer the center of Mom and Dad's world. I played second fiddle to the crying little thing. It took me a good week to adjust. I did enjoy holding her until she started to fuss or smelled bad, which was often.

Just before she was born, I was thrown out of my parents' bedroom and Terry took over my spot in the crib. The room I was sent to was small and narrow. I didn't like it because the first night in the room, I found out that I was scared of the dark. If I had to go to the bathroom, I'd hold it until morning because I didn't want to venture into the hall to use the pee pot. (We didn't have indoor plumbing at the time and a trip to the two-seater outhouse was out of the question.) I didn't know what came out after it got dark, and I didn't want to make the trip to find out.

Mom always impressed upon me the importance of watching over and protecting Terry. A tough assignment at the age of two, but I tried. I'd play close to her basket and if she smelled or began to stir too much, I'd call to Mom.

I grew to accept my new position in the family and love my sister.

Terry, as we called her, started talking very early. I acted as a go-between. I could understand what she was saying. I'd first listen to her and then tell Mom or Dad. She was seldom quiet and knew that if she asked me to get or do something for her, I'd do it. She had me wrapped around her finger and took full advantage. I learned how to say "sure" and "okay" without really listening so that I could concentrate on what I was doing at the moment.

It worked for a while, until Terry caught on to what I was up to.

Mom and Dad and the rest of the people I knew always called me Michael. Although Terry could talk a mile a minute, she had trouble with certain words. She couldn't say Michael, so she called me Gockle. It would be, "Gockle do this" or "Gockle get that." She would get me running back and forth like a madman.

I would sigh with relief when Mom would call us to the kitchen and tell us it was time for our naps.

As I lay on Mom and Dad's bed watching Terry in the crib, I'd puzzle over how Terry would go to sleep so quickly. How could she be tired? She spent most of her time in one spot giving me orders to get this or do that.

I was grateful when she had a tea party for us because it gave me a chance to sit down and pretend with her. I loved her very much and would do almost anything for her.

It's a good thing she didn't like dolls. Love can only be stretched so far.

One day we were playing by the retaining wall next to the cellar entrance at the front of the house and a big stone fell on her legs. She yelled for me to help her. Somehow I managed to lift the heavy stone and free her.

Mom thought I'd done a grand thing. Terry thought I was a hero.

I didn't think much of the act myself, but went along with the praises because I didn't get many of them.

Michael Escapes

The house came equipped with a small area of front lawn

enclosed with a wooden picket fence. I was free to leave the kitchen porch and wander in the pen.

It wasn't long before I discovered a loose picket. The bottom of it had pulled away from its nail. All I had to do was swing the bottom to one side and wiggle through. When I was free, the board would swing back to its normal position. It drove Mom crazy trying to figure out how I'd gotten out. She'd go chasing down or up the street after me and give me a sharp whack on the behind for escaping. The pain only lasted a short while and in no time I was escaping again.

She finally watched out the kitchen window while I was crawling through. Mom got a hammer and a nail, and the fence was repaired that day. My wandering days for the time being were through.

Dad Hurts Himself at Work

My escaping days were not long over when Dad came home from work at the cutlery with his hand all bandaged up in white and raised high like he was going to ask for permission to talk.

He had placed his thumb instead of a piece of steel into the press and flattened it.

We weren't living high on the hog at the time, and the accident left him out of a job for over two months. Workmen's compensation didn't pay out much to people who put their thumbs in presses. It was about twenty-seven dollars a week, which seemed like a fortune to me but not to Dad and Mom.

We were almost looking up at the belly of the hog by the time he had healed enough to go back to work. We ate supper at Grandma's house more than we usually did. Before the accident, we'd eat there on most Sundays. While Dad healed, we ate there two to three times a week.

Mr. Weeks, the Iceman

I was now old enough to store in my mind the memories of a few people who weren't related. Mr. Weeks was one of them. He was a kindly, older man. I say older because anyone over the age of ten was ancient to me. There wasn't much physically to him.

Mr. Weeks delivered a twenty-five pound block of ice to the house twice a week for our icebox. He'd carry the ice over his toweled shoulder with ice tongs. I'd hold the door open for him. He'd always smile at me and have a few happy words with Mom as he quickly went to the icebox.

He must have slept well each night after hauling blocks of ice to so many houses every day of the week except for Sundays.

The icebox had a drip pan at the bottom to collect the melted water. It became my job to empty the pan into the backyard. It wasn't much of a chore because the icebox was placed next to the outside door in the little back room. All I had to do was remove the pan, open the door, take a few steps, and give the water a toss. I got good at getting it out of the house without spilling any of the water.

Mr. Scott

Mr. Scott lived across the street from my Quigley grandparents. He had the nicest, biggest, and neatest house in Stump City. His wife had died some years ago, and he lived in the big house all alone. I don't know if he had any children. His lawn was well kept and he had flower gardens that made a good rainbow look colorless.

When he wasn't working in his lawn, he'd sit on the porch in his rocking chair reading the paper or looking at a magazine. If Grandma Quigley was on her porch, they'd exchange pleasant words. I know that he couldn't understand what Grandma was saying, but he would be polite and continue talking when she was through with her end of the conversation.

When I was old enough to play in Grandma's lawn by myself, Mr. Scott would give me an arm signal to come over to his place. If it was a hot day, he'd work the handle on the well pump in the front yard and give me a cold, delicious drink of water from the tin cup he kept on a piece of wire twisted around the faucet.

Mr. Scott would pay attention when I talked to him. His bushy, white eyebrows would furrow when I said something with a serious voice and lift ever so slightly when I said something that surprised him. We had many manly conversations about the weather, the neighbors' health, and his gardens.

I was always relaxed around him and was sad when I found out he no longer lived across the street.

Mr. Hudson, the Milkman

Mr. Hudson came to our house several times a week. He was a local farmer who operated Hudson Dairy Farm near Elbridge. He'd deliver milk to us very early in the morning. He was always neatly dressed in white with a black bowtie choking his neck. Mr. Hudson looked like a giant milk bottle with legs.

He'd arrive in a white truck, scurry up the path to the front porch, deposit the glass bottles marked in his dairy name into a silver milk cooler, pick up the cleaned empty bottles, and scurry back to his truck.

I can still hear the sound of the bottles rattling in his metal carrier as he came up to the porch and went back to his truck.

Pete the Peddler

The most exciting man to come around was Pete the Peddler. From late spring to early fall, he'd show up a few times each week. His open-air truck would be parked at the top of our road. Pete would ring a bell and the women in the neighborhood would go to his truck to buy fresh produce and chickens. They'd take the time to talk to each other and Pete sharing the latest community news. The children would walk around the truck and check out the goods.

His amazing truck had all kinds of fruits and vegetables either hanging from a board that ran around three sides of the truck or proudly displayed in slanted trays, just like Mr. Cronaeur used in his general store.

He also had chickens in cages hanging near the back tires. If a potential meal was picked out, Pete would wring the chicken's neck for the buyer and proudly hand the victim over to its new owner.

Chickens were very expensive at the time, so Mom only got one when we had a special occasion coming up in a day or two.

Pete spoke with a strong Italian accent. He was a short, skinny man with a big smile, a handlebar mustache, dark wavy hair, and fast-talking hands that he managed to keep in motion when he was filling brown bags with whatever a mother was pointing at. He'd even keep his arms moving all over the place when he was wringing a chicken's neck. The poor chicken would be flapping its wings almost as fast as Pete's arms were moving. It was a weird death dance with Pete acting as the conductor.

All of us children would watch in amazement. We were disappointed if the show wasn't done at least once a week.

Once in a while he'd give me a small piece of fruit after Mom had made her purchase. A big treat for me was a nice yellow banana.

I'd listen for his bell and go tell Mom that Pete was here. It broke up the day in a fun, exciting way. It took us a few hours to calm down after he had gone on to stir up some other neighborhood.

Mr. Cronaeur

Mr. Cronaeur owned and ran Cronaeur's General Store on Jordan Road. The railroad tracks cut across the street just before the store and then ran in front of Cowle's Chemical Company, which was right across the street from the store.

Mr. Cronaeur was a kindly, older man with white hair. Dad had worked for him before he went into the Army.

When Mom said, "Get yourself together, children, we are making a trip to the store," I'd get all excited.

Mom would have us hold onto the black baby carriage, which had become almost a permanent part of any walking trips from home, and we'd walk up the road to the store. Once we got there, Mom would put the carriage brake on, haul out whoever was it at the time, and we'd all go inside.

The store was a wonder. It had a huge cheese wheel on the counter, candy displayed in a glass enclosed case and in jars on top of the case, dry goods along the right wall, several aisles of packaged foodstuffs, a butcher shop at the back of the store, and other items on shelves behind the counter.

I don't remember what those items were because they were behind the candy. I focused on the candy.

Mr. Cronaeur would greet us with a pleasant smile and ask Mom what he could do for her. Mom would have her list in hand, glance down at it, and begin to go through the list slowly so Mr. Cronaeur had time to get each item from behind the counter. While he was getting things, Mom would tell me to get such and such from the aisles.

If we happened to need cheese, Mr. Cronaeur would cut a hunk off the wheel and weigh it. He had been doing it for so many years that the weight would be exactly right or only off by an ounce.

I had seen him cut cheese for other people and he'd always make sure the weight was right on the money as the customer watched the scale. With Mom, he was usually a bit over the weight Mom wanted.

He'd say, "Close enough, Ethel."

The blended smell of raw meat, cheese, bread, and penny candy was special.

If Mom had the money on her, she'd pay the bill. If not, Mr. Cronaeur would put it on the tab. Dad always made sure to pay the tab.

After he completed filling Mom's order and if there was nobody waiting to be served, Mr. Cronaeur would talk a bit with Mom. He'd ask how Dad was doing, talk about the weather, or tell Mom the latest news from up the road in Mottville or Skaneateles.

Before we left the store, Mr. Cronaeur would always give us some penny candy if no other children were around. He liked Dad, so he liked us.

I liked Mr. Cronaeur. Not because he gave us candy, but because he was nice to Mom.

Marty

Marty wasn't very old, but he looked it. He was considered by many in the area to be the town drunk. He lived on County Line Road and would take the shortcut across the field that led to the end of our street. He walked slowly but with grim determination past our house on his way to Rodak's Bar or some other watering hole in the area.

If I saw him coming down the road, I'd stop what I was doing and walk to the edge of the road to say hello and talk to him a little. We'd be polite to each other, but he would suddenly realize he had a mission to complete. Marty would say good-bye and walk away at a faster pace to make up for the time he lost while talking to me.

I was told that he'd never hurt a soul.

Sometimes he'd get his business done early and walk back done the road before it was dark. He'd be holding a bottle hidden in a brown bag and carry it like he had a bag full of eggs. I'd stop playing and go talk to him again. He didn't make much sense when we talked, but I felt drawn to him anyway.

This had been going on for several months and I was used to the routine. One day he came back and I went up to him with a smile on my face. For some reason, Marty grabbed onto my arm and started yelling at me. He scared and hurt me, so I yelled for Mom.

She came charging out of the house with the kitchen screen door slamming behind her. She had a scary, wild look in her eyes as she ran down the sidewalk with her apron flapping back and forth.

I knew Marty was in serious trouble because if I let the screen door slam like that, I'd get at the very least a tongue-lashing.

I've never seen a man go from one condition to another so quickly. I think Marty feared for his life. He quickly let go of my arm and started a swaying back-pedal. Mom got right in his face and began yelling at him. Poor Marty seemed to be shrinking a bit closer to the road with every word. I stood there with my jaw dropped, crying.

Mom was using words that she had never used before. Words that would have had my teeth rubbed with a bar of soap.

When it was over, Marty was moving very fast and almost in a straight line down the road toward home.

Mom watched him move away for a bit. Then she turned to me and told me to never get near him again.

That turned out to be no problem because if Marty did his drinking in the day, he no longer took the short cut down our road. He took the long way up County Line Road and then down Stump Road

When Dad found out about what Marty had done to me, he was upset but not angry. Both his voice and eyes were sad as he told me to stay clear of him.

Dad knew something else about Marty, but he didn't tell me.

One night I looked out the bedroom window when I heard a dog barking. It was Marty going by our house. He wasn't walking at his normal, slow speed, and he kept looking at our house to see if Mom was going to come out after him.

It dumbfounded me that he'd risk his life to save a few minutes' walking time. He must have been very late for an appointed time with The Drink.

The Olmsteads

Dad had been working Saturdays for Johnny Olmstead on Mrs. Olmstead's dairy farm. Mrs. Olmstead and her late husband had taken Johnny in when he was a youngster. He was a hard-working man and kept the farm neat and in the black.

Dad would help with the plowing, planting, harvesting, feeding, and milking. One Saturday I spent the whole day working with Dad picking stones in a big field. I had fun riding on the stone bolt and throwing on what I could handle while Dad picked on the bigger stones. It was hard labor for a man of almost four, but I loved being outdoors with my father and working. I think Dad paid me either a dime or a quarter for helping him for the day.

Johnny would let me feed and water the calves while he and Dad did the milking. I like the mixed smells of hay, straw, milk, cow, and manure. I could almost hear a pleasant, soft tune coming from the blend of cows chewing hay, milk machines pumping, straw rustling, and milk splashing into a pail as Dad milked a cow that was afraid of the noisy milking machine.

It was all very good.

Mrs. Olmstead was very old and blind. She smelled like a mix of sauce, spices, yeast, and bread flour. She was a wonderful cook and gave me a cookie or two during my few ventures into her ancient home.

The house was filled with very old furniture, a huge spinning wheel, dark pictures and paintings. Smaller things were placed on shelves, tables, desks, and drawers. The oldness of the stuff almost overpowered the smell of the freshly baked cookies. It was a warm, comforting mix.

I wondered how she managed to do all she did in the huge house without being able to see and with not one light on until Johnny or Dad turned a switch.

Fiddler Bin

I never met Fiddler Bin, but Dad told me about him. He lived just up the road in a small shack. He was a Spanish-American War soldier. He came back to Stump City and set up camp in the small woods just off County Line Road. He didn't work and lived on his small army pension and handouts from the folks who lived nearby. Bathing was out of the question as far as Bin was concerned.

We had something in common when it came to water.

Fiddler Bin drank up most of his pension money to forget what happened to him and his army friends during some battle.

He was a good fiddler. The people in Stump City could hear him play, especially at night. Once in a while he'd get up the courage to play at some special outdoor event. He'd be placed downwind of the celebration to keep his smell from driving people away.

When the memories that haunted him came back too strongly, he'd howl like a crazy man while he played his fiddle. His eerie cries could be heard all over Stump City.

He got very sick, so some of the men in Stump City loaded him into the back of a truck and took him to the hospital. The doctor wouldn't examine him until he got cleaned up. He was kicking and screaming when he caught on to what was happening. When he hit the water, he died instantly.

Sometimes I'd think of Fiddler Bin when I climbed into the washtub and wondered if I'd come out alive or dead. Like Fiddler Bin, my body didn't take to being too clean.

Several years later when I was allowed to wander further from home, I went to the woods where Fiddler Bin had built his shack. I found a pile of rotted wood, rusted tin plates and cups, but no fiddle.

I was a little scared to be there. I'd look over my shoulder once in a while to see if Bin's ghost was behind me.

I felt sorry for Fiddler Bin.

More on *Aunt Pat and Uncle Danny*

Close to the time I had the scary meeting with Marty, Aunt Pat and Uncle Danny returned to Stump City. They came back with their first-born, a boy named John who was almost the same age as Terry.

They bought Mr. Scott's house, because he had become feeble and had to go live somewhere else.

I missed him, and I knew he missed his gardens. At least I could still get water from the well.

Uncle Danny worked as a traveling salesman. He sold china place settings and would be gone for a day or two at a time. He had a big garage built by the house and stored tons and tons of china in there.

I was sternly warned not to venture into the garage without an adult being with me. I never broke many things at home and couldn't figure out their great concern.

Aunt Pat got a job teaching at a school in Auburn. Aunt

Mary and Aunt Ann would take care of John while she was working.

I kept looking for signs that Aunt Mary had gotten to John. But I never saw the hint of a nervous twitch or him constantly looking over his shoulder. I think Aunt Ann kept him away from Aunt Mary most of the time. That's the only way I can figure out why he was normal.

Mom told me it must be "Divine Intervention."

Why did Aunt Pat and Uncle Danny want to come back and live right across the street from Grandma and Grandpa? Aunt Mary lived there too! Maybe they both had memory problems and forgot how she acted, or maybe Aunt Mary was mellowing as she got older. She sure hadn't smoothed out any of her rough edges when it came to me.

Shortly before Terry turned two, Mom's belly seemed to be getting big. To compound my puzzlement, Aunt Pat's belly was too, and she was always thin before. Mom wasn't as trim as Aunt Pat, but she wasn't eating any more than she usually did.

Patty

Patricia Ann showed up in the world just before the summer of 1950. I remember seeing her for the first time in the hospital. Her beautiful, blond hair was in sharp contrast to the white sheet she was sleeping on. It was amazing to me that she was not crying. Maybe I caught her in a good moment.

The Five-Day Vacation Theory, Part I

Baby doctors required new mothers to stay in the hospital for five days. It seemed to be the right amount of time. I knew then that babies came out of their moms' tummies through the belly button. It would take time and effort for a baby to come out that way, seeing how a baby is much bigger than a belly button. It probably would take even more time for the moms' belly buttons to heal.

Aunt Ann Helps

Aunt Ann came to the house to care for Dad, Terry, and me. She treated us well and cooked for us.

According to strict Irish standards, Dad's only job in the kitchen was to get in there in time for a prepared meal and leave when we were all done. He carried on the tradition with great skill even when Aunt Ann was there to help.

Aunt Ann would come in the morning just before Dad had to leave for work. We'd have fun playing with her and would get her laughing over silly little things.

One time I talked in a serious voice about how I believed babies were born. She laughed until she almost cried. This puzzled me a great deal. How could she laugh at something that had to be very painful for women to go through?

Aunt Ann would stay until after Dad got home. She'd eat with us, clean up the kitchen, get Terry and me ready for bed, and then leave for the night.

I liked saying my bedtime prayers with Dad because he always got down on his knees with us while Terry and I prayed. He'd have his head bowed and would rub his hands together as if he was trying to keep them warm. After we prayed, he'd tuck us in and give us a goodnight kiss.

The Kitchen

Doing dishes and cleaning up the kitchen was a chore because we didn't have running hot water. Mom would have to get a kettle on the boil and pour it into the freestanding porcelain sink. I don't know how she stuck her hands into the water. I tried it once and quickly pulled my hand out.

The kitchen was small. The sink was on one wall with a door to the right. The door opened to the back room where the icebox was located. The gas stove was against the wall next to the sink. The cupboard was between the pantry door and the entrance to the small living room. It reached to the ceiling and had doors at the bottom for storing pots and pans. (It was my favorite hiding spot when Terry and I played Hide and Go Seek.) The kitchen table took up most of the floor space. In a pinch, it would seat six.

The gas stove was small but a monster. Many times Mom would lose arm hairs when she fired up the oven. It required a lit, rolled-up piece of paper to get started. Mom had to turn on the gas and immediately stick the lit paper towards the bottom-back of the oven. If she wasn't quick enough, the gas would be too much and there'd be a giant "whooshing" sound. Mom would squeal, jump back, and examine her arm. She was almost as afraid of the stove as I was.

I always watched her light it when I was around. If Mom was going to get blown up, I wanted to go with her.

Patty and Mom Come Home

The day Pat and Mom got home, Terry got kicked out of the folks' bedroom. She got the front bedroom all to herself. It was huge by my standards and had two windows instead of one like mine, and she had a much more interesting view than I had. She could watch the activity on the road, see part of the dam, the ruins of the old button works, and the woods, and watch the workers going back and forth in the windows of the Welch Allyn factory across the creek. From my window I could just see over the top of the hill, the shed, and the outhouse.

My baby sister Pat didn't cry much. She would whine and fuss a bit if she was hungry or needed changing. Mom knew if Pat cried, she had to be either sick or teething. She was no problem at all for Mom.

Dad seemed to like her a lot more than Terry and me, maybe because she was so cute or because she didn't cause the problems that we did. She was a very special baby to us all.

I don't remember being jealous of her—much.

The Five-Day Vacation Theory, Part II

Aunt Pat had another baby shortly after Mom came home from the hospital with Patty. She was named Mary Kay.

I think Aunt Pat planned it this way, so she could get fresher news from Mom about how the hospital worked the five-day vacation. After all, it was at least two years since Mom or Aunt Pat had been there and any mom could forget a lot about the five-day vacation after that long.

Moms liked to take five-day vacations at the hospital. I think they all wanted to get out of their houses because they had to work so hard and used having babies as a good excuse to fly the coop for a breather. Why not? They could sleep all they wanted and they had nurses in white uniforms waiting on them hand and foot. Moms can be very smart.

The smartest woman in Stump City by a long shot was Mrs. Walton. She had gone on seven five-day vacations, and she was wearing a baggy shirt again. She had figured out the system quicker than any woman I ever knew.

The vacations also made their husbands appreciate them more. You see, the men were used to meals being prepared for them at a set time, having their clothes ironed a certain way, and having their homes cleaned regularly. The Home System was thrown into a tizzy during the five-day vacations. The men would be relieved when the natural order of things returned when their wives got home.

One of Mom's friends was in the kitchen talking to her shortly after Pat was born. She didn't know I was under the table looking at a picture book about Robin Hood. She quietly told Mom that she was going to have another baby.

Then she whispered in a lower voice, "Ethel, this will teach him for keeping me up late so many nights." She and Mom giggled in a very knowing way.

Her words made me wonder if there wasn't another reason for all the five-day vacations. Were some of the moms mad at their husbands for keeping them up late and just wanted to get away from them to cool off? What did nights have to do with babies?

The whole five-day vacation thing was confusing me and hurting my head. I knew I was missing something, but couldn't figure out what it was. I went back to only half-looking at Robin Hood pictures. I wished I was smarter.

More about Aunt Mary and Uncle Bob

On a Saturday morning I walked into the kitchen shortly after Uncle Jimmy left. He had talked quietly to Mom and Dad in a serious tone. I was surprised to see Dad crying while he rested his right arm against the kitchen window. Mom was standing over the kitchen sink with her hands over her eyes.

I walked over to Mom, and she quietly told me that Uncle Bob had died while shaving.

Did he cut his leg while sharpening his razor or slit his throat when he was stretching his neck skin? I had watched Dad and Grandpa shave many times. They always had close calls and ended up with pieces of toilet paper on the bleeding spots.

I felt sorry for Dad and wanted to hug him, but I was bigger now and didn't. I helplessly went over and stood by him. He took his right arm off the windowsill and began to stroke my back while he cried.

When Dad calmed down some, he told me that Uncle Bob always had a weak heart, and he had died of a heart attack.

It was the first I saw Dad cry. I didn't see him cry again for many more years.

I now knew why Uncle Bob hadn't joined the Army with Dad.

I didn't mention anything to either Mom or Dad about the wake and it wasn't brought up. I was relieved. The thought of seeing Uncle Bob dead scared me.

Aunt Mary's frenzy for activity became even greater after Uncle Bob had passed. She busied herself around her parents' house and moved back in with them even before the trailer was sold.

Poor Aunt Ann and Uncle Jimmy!

Once in awhile I'd see Aunt Mary crying in the kitchen. One time I got up enough nerve to go over to her and give her a hug. She hugged me back and cried all the more.

I could never understand Aunt Mary.

Pete Cashin and Davy Walton

When I was getting close to the age of five, Mom would let

me wander a bit further away from home. I followed Pete Cashin and Davy Walton when they would let me, but I kept myself in the background. They were two or three years older than I was and much bigger. They both lived on Stump Road. I didn't do much with them, but it was nice just to be in the presence of older men and away from the women at home.

Once school started, I'd sneak up by the fence close to where they got on the bus and watch them get on board. It seemed like a long time before the bus came back in the afternoon. I would wait the proper length of time and then go play with one of them for a while if nothing else was going on for them to do.

Pete raised chickens for his Dad. Once I was there when his Dad told Pete four of them had to be killed for some customers.

Pete and I chased the chickens until we caught and caged them. Pete then brought the victims over to the chopping block one at a time. I held each chicken tightly by the head while Pete held it by the legs and stretched it out over the chopping block. He'd then pick up the hatchet and chop off its head. When he let go of the chicken's legs, it either ran around a little or took off flying on its final flight.

After we killed all four, Mrs. Cashin plucked all of them, cut them open, and gutted them.

I was fascinated by the whole thing but didn't like the smell of chicken guts.

Mary McEneny's Wake

During the hot summer, Big Jim McEneny's wife, Mary, died. Big Jim was John's brother and lived in the small house next to Aunt Pat and Uncle Danny.

Big Jim and Mary used to live on Vinegar Hill Road. He had a small farm there. They bought Grandpa and Grandma

Quigley's house when the Quigley family got too big for it. The house was the right size for the McEnenys because they didn't have any children. Mary McEneny was a very nice lady and often gave me one of her wonderful cookies.

Dad and his sisters and brother were born in the house right next door to Big Jim's house many years earlier during a time when doctors didn't think moms needed five-day vacations.

The day after O'Neill's Funeral Home in Skaneateles had tidied up and beautified Big Jim's wife, Dad had to almost drag me to Big Jim's house for the wake. I knew I had to go, but I was really scared. Dad figured I was old enough to see a dead person and get a taste of an Irish wake.

I wasn't in a tasting mood, but I didn't have a choice.

There was a long line of people waiting outside to go see and pray for her for the last time. It gave me many extra minutes to imagine a dead body. Some older boy, more than likely Pete Cashin, had told me that a body would move once in a while and make strange noises from the belly area. He said that a body even could make moaning noises. I kept thinking about these facts while we waited. It was hot enough out as it was, but I could really feel the sweat dripping down my face now. The tie, which Dad said was thought up by the French to torture the rest of the world for all its defeats in wars, didn't help either.

We finally got into the house and I peeked around the corner. The sight set me back a bit and I would have turned and run if Dad didn't have a hand on my shoulder.

People in the kitchen and dining room were eating, drinking, and laughing as if they were separated from the body by a block or two.

I wasn't hungry at all, which by Mom's standards meant I was catching, or had, a bug.

We got to shake Big Jim's gorilla hand. I mumbled something to him and kept a sharp eye on his wife while Dad talked to him. She didn't look too bad for being dead.

I was looking and listening for any of the things the older boy had told me a dead person could do. I really got scared when I thought I saw one of her fingers move.

After Dad finished talking to Big Jim, we went to the kneeling bench right in front of the casket. The room was very hot and the smell of the flowers was almost too much for my nose to take. I said the quickest prayer of my life and waited for Dad to finish his. I kept my eyes shut now and began to pray for Dad. It was a prayer to make his prayers go quicker.

After what seemed like an hour, he finished and we went into the dining room. He handed me a soda, and he had some good Irish whiskey—the kind saved for only weddings and funerals. I didn't hear a word Dad was saying because I was looking at the doorway that went into the living room. I was certain that Big Jim's wife was about to stick her head around the corner to see who was eating, drinking, and messing up her dining room.

I was as uncomfortable as a wounded rabbit waiting for the cat to pounce.

Dad ate just a cookie and then had two shots of the good whiskey to wash it down. The only thing that saved me was Dad had to get back home to watch Terry, Pat, and me while Mom came up to pay her respects.

Mom was awfully brave to go up there by herself. She probably didn't have all the facts about what dead people could do.

As Mom would say, "Ignorance is bliss."

Dad Becomes a Public Servant

Dad passed the New York State Civil Service Test. He had

studied long and hard for it earlier in the year. Soon after he got his test score, he started a job in Auburn examining unemployment claims.

He exchanged his work clothes for a tie. The new job freed him from the cutlery work and probably saved him a finger or two.

He no longer came home all tired out and dirty.

Grandpa Simpson

It was early in 1951 when Mom got a letter from her only sister, Madge. Mom was crying and holding the letter. Grandpa Simpson was dead. He had been in great pain for several days and refused to go to the doctor. Grandpa had a strangulated hernia.

I didn't exactly know what it meant, but I wouldn't want to be strangled on any part of my body.

Mom often talked about him with love in her voice and eyes. He was a cabinetmaker, and our house had several articles of furniture that he had made and sent to us. All the items were done with hand tools from scrap oak left over from furniture he had made for people. They were beautiful.

Mom would spend lots of time polishing each one. Sometimes she'd have tears in her eyes while she was polishing.

I knew at these moments she missed Grandpa and England because the wood brought good memories back to her about him and Ellesmere.

I felt very sorry for Mom and held her around the waist while she cried her heart out. I was also crying. I knew that she loved him very much.

Even though I had never met him, I loved him because of what Mom had told me about him.

She had now lost her major tie to England because she never said much about Grandma Simpson or her sister Madge.

The Holstein Cows

Dad always liked farm work and decided that he could make some extra money for the house by getting Holstein milk cows. He bought three of them from Mrs. Olmstead and kept them on the Olmstead farm. The farm was about two miles from home. Dad would have to get up very early in the morning to milk them. When he got home from his regular job, he'd have to change and go back to the farm to milk them again. He sold most of the milk to Mrs. Olmstead to feed her calves. The rest he'd bring home for us.

Mom invested in a hand-crank butter churn. It had a red top with a crank handle and wooden paddles that madly spun around inside the glass container when the crank was turned.

Terry and I thought it was great fun to make butter. After a few months the excitement wore off. The butter sure tasted good, so I focused on the end product and not the chore. The rich, creamy butter was much better than the greasy, cheap oleo that was used before the cows.

Dad kept the cows for about a year, which seemed like a long time considering all the work they were.

It was back to oleo.

Entertainment

We had a small tabletop radio encased with wood. It was our main source of entertainment. Terry and I liked to listen to shows like *The Lone Ranger*, *The Buster Brown Show*, *Fibber Magee and Molly*, and *Roy Rogers and Dale Evans*.

On Friday night I was allowed to listen to the *Friday Night Fights* with Dad. That was a lot of fun. Dad's love for boxing drew him to listen to the pros fight. His two favorites were Rocky Marciano and Carman Basillio.

When I listened, I could almost see the boxers taking swings at each other. If I didn't know what was going on, Dad would explain during commercials.

The Gillette Razor Company was the main sponsor. I can still here the Gillette jingle:

"To look sharp and to feel sharp too..."

Saturday and Bath Day

Saturday was the best day of the week. We didn't have school and could play all day after the Saturday morning kids' shows. If the weather was good, we'd spend the whole afternoon playing outside.

There was one thing, though, that would enter my mind and take the edge off Saturday's fun. Saturday was also the day for our weekly baths. I didn't mind washing my hands and face too much, but the baths made me feel a little like Fiddler Bin must have felt when he was forced into the tub at the hospital.

Mom would get hot water going on the stove and clean pajamas out. She would wash us up in a metal tub placed on the storage room floor. She'd have a few towels underneath it to keep the floor dry. After each shivering child climbed out, the water would be a bit cool. Mom would get more hot water off the kitchen stove and pour it into the tub, and the next victim would climb in. The water temperature was either too hot or too cold. The cleanest one would be the child picked first for a bath. I think I was usually last because I got the dirtiest during the week. I don't think a dog would drink the water after I got through. I rarely felt very clean after a bath.

In the winter the bath was a cold affair. The only thing that saved us was the coal burning stove in the living room and clean, well-worn Dr. Denton's. We'd finish drying off standing as close to the stove as we could.

The coal stove was our source of heat. The only two rooms that stayed warm on cold winter days were the living room and Terry's bedroom. Her room was directly over the living room and the stovepipe ran up through it. The rest of the house varied in temperature depending on the wind. The windier it got, the colder the rest of the house became.

Michael Starts School

In the fall of 1951, I finally got to go to school. I was all excited about riding on the bus with Pete and Davy. The excitement soon wore off. I found out that I got bus sick easily. I didn't like school and would rather be playing outside. Kindergarten only lasted the morning, so I was a free man the rest of the day.

Mrs. Peck was my teacher. She was a short, plump, nice lady. I frequently got into trouble. There was a bathroom in our room and one day she had to use it. It must have been some type of big emergency for her because the only time she would go in there was when a kid asked for help getting his clothes back in the right position. When she came out I said real loudly in front of the class, "Mrs. Peck, did you have to go pee?"

We didn't have a phone, so I don't know how Mom found out so fast about it. She scolded me for speaking out like that. Mom was trying to hold back a laugh when she was talking to me, but she didn't do too well.

I noticed that Mom was putting on weight again. She soon started wearing baggy shirts to hide the bigger belly. There was a connection, but I couldn't quite put my finger on it.

Was it because Dad kept Mom up late and she was getting even?

Indoor Plumbing

In the fall, Dad began digging a hole by the side of the house. It was a big project and took several afternoons after he got home from work to complete. He said it was for a septic tank. I had to ask him what that was. I got all excited when he told me that it was needed when people had toilets and bathtubs in their houses. Most of our neighbors now had toilets inside with a bathtub in the same room, and I wanted them too.

One day I came flying around the back of the house and went headlong into the hole. I let out a scream as I went down. It didn't hurt much. I had a heck of a time trying to climb up the straight walls.

Mom heard me and came running out to rescue me. At least the metal tank wasn't in and the hole was dry. I imagined the other possible scene and I shuddered. Dad put some boards over the hole when he got home from work.

A week or so after the hole was big enough and the tank was installed, Mr. Manley came to the house. He was a giant of a man with big hams for hands. He was carrying a huge, wooden tool kit. It must have weighed fifty pounds. He held it in his hand as if it were part of his body and not some great weight. He didn't even bother to put it down while he talked to Dad. He was the local plumber.

I watched Mr. Manley work. He was doing a lot of puttering just to put a toilet and tub in. I didn't know that a hot water heater had to be installed. I thought a hot water pipe was just that and something fancy wasn't needed to warm the water.

The job was done. I test-drove the toilet and it worked just fine. We no longer had the trip to the smelly two-seater.

Dad was also spared the terrible job of cleaning out the pit. He'd use a shovel and buckets and throw the smelly contents onto the garden. I stayed away as far as possible. I didn't want to carry the buckets to the garden.

It was a big day of technological advancement for the whole family, especially for Dad.

The secondhand, white cast iron tub had short legs with some type of animal foot design on them. I tried to picture it walking around the house, but I couldn't.

I no longer dreaded the Saturday night bath—except for feeling very cold when I got out of the tub and thinking about what happened to Fiddler Bin.

More about School

I was getting settled into school now. I really liked to draw and paint. Playtime was fun too. The naps were boring because I could never catch a wink. I think they were put into the program to give Mrs. Peck a break. She needed one with kids like me pestering her and running around all the time.

Today there is some fancy doctor name for what I had. Mom's medicine for the ailment was an occasional placement over her knee. The medicine seemed to work rather well. I'd be good for a stretch until the memory of the medicine wore off. Mom would give me another dose and I'd be good as new again.

Mrs. Peck appreciated the medicine that I got at home.

Sledding

Terry and I were now old enough to go sledding on the hill that ran down the side of our house. We'd have a great time going down. If the snow was fast, we'd even be able to get across the road, when Mom was busy with Pat and didn't see what we were doing, and zip down the trail that led to the base of the dam. We didn't worry about cars because the road was very quiet.

John

In the spring of 1952, Mom took another five-day vacation. She was really taking advantage of them and seemed to be determined to catch up with Mrs. Walton, a mighty challenge indeed.

For the third time, Aunt Ann was placed in charge of our care and feeding. She was still fun to have in the house. We liked the change, but we still missed Mom.

Two days after our new baby brother was born, we went with Dad to visit Mom in the hospital. We first went to the baby nursery. Dad asked us to pick out our brother. He had already told us that John was very small. We all picked out the right baby. All we had to do was look for the smallest baby in there.

Baby John looked scrawny. He had dark, thick hair and cried weakly. His skin had an off color too.

I was worried about him.

After looking at him for a few minutes, we went to visit Mom. She looked very comfortable in the bed and had a nurse helping her. She gave us all hugs and kisses and we talked.

It wasn't long until she said that she was tired and needed some sleep.

Sleep! It was only 4:30 in the afternoon.

I could tell that this was one of the better points of the five-day vacations that moms took advantage of before they came home with a new baby.

No wonder Mom and her friend were chuckling in the kitchen.

Moms are not only smart, they are very sneaky.

I knew that the front bedroom was going to start to get crowded. Boy, was Pat in for a surprise. Someone else would be taking her place for attention, and she'd have to move out of her sleeping quarters with Mom and Dad.

Pat moved in with Terry. She settled in very quickly and with very little fuss.

This was a strange way for her to behave because I didn't like it at all when I got kicked out and thought she wouldn't either.

Pat was almost two at the time of her room exchange. I couldn't find any fault with her, except she liked to play with dolls, which puzzled Terry and me. She wasn't demanding and became Mom's little helper. She'd sit on Dad's lap and laugh when he bounced her on his knee singing "Home again, home again Jiggidy did." Her long, braided hair would be bouncing up and down too.

It was fun to watch.

Terry and I got our turns too, but they didn't last as long because we were much bigger than Patty.

I learned early that the smaller brother or sister got more attention from Mom and Dad.

John came home with Mom. He was very tiny and had very skinny arms and legs.

Will Mom place him in a box and put him in the stove like Grandma Quigley did with Aunt Ann? I was dying to see how the system worked.

John took up a lot of Mom's time. She'd fuss over him and seemed very concerned about his health. She would just say that he needed time to grow. All of us handled him very carefully. She never did put him in the stove.

I was disappointed. John wasn't.

He had feet that turned in. Mom said they were clubfeet. I couldn't see how they looked like clubs. They just looked like they were turned in a bit too much, as if he practiced trying to keep his big toes close together while keeping his heels as far away from each other as possible.

When John was a bit older, Mom and Dad took him to a foot specialist. When they got home, John had two heavy casts that went almost up to his knees. When he crawled across the bare floor, the casts would make loud thudding sounds. He was easy to keep track of. If the thuds were missing, Mom would send one of us to see what John was doing. Quiet children who are on the loose usually mean trouble.

John's arms got very strong from pulling the extra weight around. One time when Mom and I were in the kitchen, there was a very loud thud that shook the ceiling. It came from Mom and Dad's bedroom above. Mom and I ran up the stairs to see what had happened. John was sitting on the floor with a big grin on his face. How did he get out of the crib?

The next time he was put in the crib, Mom spied on him like she had spied on me when I escaped from the fenced-in area. She watched as John pulled himself up the bars to the railing and lifted himself up until his arms were straight. Then he got himself swinging from side to side. When his legs got high enough, he made a final push with his arms and flew out of the crib.

Mom got to him just before he hit the floor.

I thought it was amazing. Mom didn't. John didn't either when he got spanked.

The ceiling didn't shake after that.

The End of Kindergarten

Somehow Mrs. Peck didn't fail me in kindergarten. There was talk in the class and on the bus toward the end of the year that she had failed kids before. I was really worried about it. Mom would have thrown a fit and put me in the bedroom for the whole summer. I breathed a sigh of relief when I found out that I was going into first grade.

I decided then and there that school was easy, and I didn't have to do much to pass. Mrs. Peck was the only kindergarten teacher. There could have been something to this, but I couldn't figure it out.

Grandma Simpson

Sometime during the summer, Mom got another letter from her sister, Aunt Madge. I watched her read the letter. The more she read, the redder she got. When she was done she stood there shaking while she tore the letter into little pieces.

In the letter Aunt Madge explained that she and Uncle Frank could not take in Grandma Simpson. She said that they couldn't afford the extra expense and their cottage was just too small. She wanted Mom and Dad to take Grandma Simpson. Madge said that she would pay for Grandma's ship ticket.

In earlier letters, Madge had said that she and Uncle Frank were just doing fine. She was working as a secretary, and Uncle Frank was continuing the same work he had during the war as a plane engineer.

How could they not afford to keep Grandma with them?

I felt some tension between Mom and Dad because of the letter. The little house was beginning to complain and starting to come apart at the seams with four kids, and money being a scarce thing.

How could the house hold another person who would need a separate room?

Mom finally talked Dad into letting Grandma come to live with us. Grandma Simpson would soon sail on the *Queen Mary* from Liverpool to New York City.

There were lots of changes made before Grandma arrived. The biggest immediate one was my removal from the small, back bedroom. I got moved to the front bedroom. Terry and Pat had one side of the room and I got the other.

At least I had more things to see out the window when I got sent to the room for some minor rule infraction.

I felt braver having Terry and Pat sleeping in the same room. I now got up to use the pee pot instead of holding on until morning. I wasn't brave enough yet to venture downstairs to use the toilet.

One night I got up to go and was more asleep than awake. Instead of peeing in the pee pot, I filled one of Dad's new, expensive Nettleton shoes. I really got in trouble the next morning when Dad went to put on the shoe.

Mom had a heck of a time getting it dried out and suitable

for wear. The shoes cost Dad a few days' wages and they were not going to be thrown out.

I made sure that I went in the pee pot from then on.

Grandma Simpson

About a week before Grandma Simpson came, Mom spent many hours painting my old room. She also got some nice second-hand furniture and pictures to help Grandma feel welcome and comfortable.

When we met her for the first time, my sisters and I gave her polite hugs.

While Grandma talked to Mom in the kitchen, I looked her over. She was short and her belly stuck out. From what little I could see of her legs, they didn't look like they could support the weight they had to carry around. Black wire-rimmed glasses made her eyes look big because the glass in them was thick. When she turned so that I could see her from the side, I noticed that she had a hump on her back. It made her look like a picture of a witch I had once seen. Her gray hair was in a bun and held in place by some type of black netting. She lifted an arm to point at something on top of the cupboard, and I noticed that the skin on her underarm was wrinkled and flabby.

She talked to Mom with a commanding, crackling voice. Most of the time she would ask one question after another without waiting for Mom to answer any of them.

After politely listening to Grandma talk on for several minutes, Dad excused himself and went outside to get Grandma's luggage. He didn't look at all happy.

I continued to stand there while Grandma went on talking to Mom as if none of us children were in the room.

Terry went into the living room and came back into the kitchen carrying John.

Grandma turned to see who had interrupted her.

She stared at John for a moment before she took him out of Terry's arms.

She held him at arm's length and said, "This poor, scrawny child won't live long."

After giving John a quick hug, Grandma shook her head and handed him back to Terry.

Mom got a worried look on her face.

I could tell that she was about to say something to Grandma because she looked at her and opened her mouth. Instead, she closed it, turned to us and said, "Children, go outside and play."

As I went outside, I started thinking about what Grandma had said about John. In the past Mom told me that Grandma had three of her children die at a very young age.

Grandma must know what she was talking about when it comes to the health of little ones.

I hadn't worried about John since shortly after he got out of the hospital because I had gotten used to how he looked and acted.

John seemed healthy to me, but after what Grandma had said, I started to look at him closely to see if there were any signs he'd die on us real soon.

It took all of us a long time to get used to having Grandma living with us. The house was never again the same. It was not only very crowded, but we had another mother to watch us and correct us when we did something wrong.

She never warmed up to me nor did I warm up to her. I

don't think I measured up to what she thought a "proper" boy should be. Boys must have behaved very differently in England.

She had a special drawer in her bedroom that held penny candies. She gave them out to well-behaved children. Pat got a lot of candy. I don't remember getting any. I never saw Terry walking out of Grandma's room with a piece of candy either, and Terry wasn't close to being as bad as I was.

I don't think Dad liked Grandma because he never had much to say to her. Oh, he was polite because he was brought up to respect his elders, but he didn't go out of his way to strike up a conversation.

Grandma didn't either.

With three little ones, me, and Grandma Simpson in the house, it was a tough time for Dad to bring in enough money for us to survive. Grandma got a very small pension check from England once a month, but it wasn't enough to help.

The Drink

To make matters worse, Dad's case of the Irish Disease was growing. He would work hard all week and on the weekends spend some of the necessary money for our survival on "The Drink." I didn't know much then, but sensed there was a grand tension building between Mom and Dad.

If Dad came home from a bar before we were in bed, Mom would get us upstairs before Dad got into the house. She didn't want us to see Dad in "The Condition."

There would be arguments in the kitchen with Mom doing a great deal of crying. The walls were thin and the house was small. Not much escaped my ears. Grandma's name would often come up.

Grandma didn't leave her room when Dad came home drunk.

After a day or night of drinking, Dad would have a terrible headache the next morning and make frequent visits to the bathroom to empty his stomach. He would stay in bed until the afternoon.

Mom would not be on speaking terms with him for several days. It bothered Terry and me, but we didn't speak about it. Pat just continued playing with her dolls as if nothing was wrong.

I sided with Mom and ignored Dad to punish him for spending money foolishly.

The house would settle down to being near normal until Dad went on another tour of the bars.

It was a routine that I could never get used to.

I don't remember him ever missing much work. Dad tried hard to keep his drinking to the weekends.

Because Dad was peeing money down the toilet, Mom had to feed us less. For supper we'd eat lots of potatoes with just a hint of some cheap meat to flavor the spuds.

It's a good thing that I liked peanut butter and jelly sandwiches for lunch because that is what I'd have most of the time.

A Contradiction

Some of the best times I had with Dad as a youngster were when he'd go out for something and take me along. Many times we'd end up at Murray's Bar in Hartlot. The place fascinated me. There was sawdust on the floor with spittoons placed where the men could easily reach them with their accurate spitting. The loud-talking and sometimes-singing men brought light into the dimly-lit, high-ceilinged bar. The wonderful smell of beer covered over the smell of unwashed men.

Most of the men knew Dad, so I was accepted. Dad would let me sip some foam from the top of his beer. It was delicious and didn't taste a bit like shaving cream. (Yes, I did try it one time. Not good.)

When I was with him, Dad didn't come home drunk. It was a happy time because Dad would play with us and sing silly songs. He didn't play with us much unless he was a bit into the bottle.

A Very Bad Day

If Dad had too much to drink and came home early on Saturday, we'd stay away from him by playing outside because he wasn't Dad. He'd change from a kind, soft-spoken person to someone we didn't know or want to know.

The worst time we had with The Drink happened on a Saturday afternoon. Dad came home fully armed and loaded for bear. He had mentioned how bad the English treated the Irish on previous returns from the bars, but this time he was really angry. Grandma Simpson headed for her room and locked her door. We huddled in the other room. It was loud in the kitchen.

Dad kept asking, "Where's Michael?"

When Dad stumbled out to the car to get something, Mom came to us with fear written all over her face. She quietly told me to take Terry, Pat, and John over to the McEneny house next door by sneaking out our back door.

We got to the McEneny house without Dad noticing by going behind our house where there was no window for Dad to look out and see what we were doing.

All four of us were very scared because Mom was acting scared and Dad was acting like a madman.

We huddled in the kitchen. Mrs. McEneny told us in a firm voice to be quiet and stay away from any windows.

We sat at the kitchen table, and Mrs. McEneny gave us cookies and milk to calm us down some.

A good cookie always helped me to settle down, but it didn't help much this time.

Of course, I had to look out once in a while when Mrs. McEneny turned her back or left the room. After some time, I saw Dad go to the burn barrel behind the house with papers and a can of gasoline. When Dad lit the papers, a blast of fire and hot air hit him. He almost fell over backwards, and he quickly retreated back to the house.

After what seemed like a very long time, Mom came. She was shaking and crying. She told us that it was safe to come home now because Dad had taken the car and gone.

I figured Dad, in his drunken condition, had planned on taking out all his hatred toward the English on me. I was really scared.

When I was in bed that night, I tried to stay awake to hear him coming home. I fell asleep waiting. I don't know what I would have done if he had come home when I was awake.

"The Drink" is a terrible thing.

Me and The Drink

Dad would try to quit and go for several months without a drop. Then something would happen to start him up again. The cycle would be repeated many times.

Even when Dad was dry as a bone, I'd wonder when he'd start drinking again.

When he was out drinking, I'd lie awake in bed until he got home, I'd heard the kitchen door open and then close, and he'd gotten into bed.

I worried about him being in a car wreck before he got home, and then I worried that something terrible would happen when he did get home.

The relief and then the fear were not good for me. I was getting more than my share of upset stomachs.

Grandma Simpson Goes to Work

Grandma Simpson learned from one of her friends at church about an older woman who needed someone to live in her house and take care of her.

Grandma would get room and board plus a small amount of money each week and have Sundays off.

Mom and Dad really liked the idea and told her to take the job.

It would be nice not to have her watching me all the time. When she left, the house seemed to breathe a sigh of relief.

I sure did!

Her first job lasted about two months. The old woman she was staying with died putting Grandma out of work.

Did she die of natural causes, or did Grandma quicken her exit from this earth?

There were lots of old women in the area, so Grandma's services were in great demand. It wasn't long before she was off to another old lady's home.

Harry Joyce

Once a year, Harry Joyce would come to visit. He and Dad were best friends when they were in the Army and stationed together in England. Mr. Joyce was even my godfather. When I found out that he was coming, I'd get all excited and happy.

Mr. Joyce was a bachelor and seemed to have lots of money. He wore nice clothes all the time, drove a shiny convertible, and always came with presents for each of us children and Mom. He treated Mom with great respect, like a lady, and could get her to smile and laugh—a remarkable feat.

Making Mom feel special and happy were Mr. Joyce's best presents.

I'd sit and listen quietly as he and Dad talked. I don't remember the conversations, but do remember the amazing change he made in Dad. I could almost see the tension in Dad's face disappear.

It was good to see this change in Dad.

Dad would drink with Mr. Joyce while they talked, but I don't really remember either one of them getting drunk to the mad point.

Oh, it was so exciting to see Dad act like how I thought a normal father should act. I wished that Mr. Joyce would never leave the house. I think my sisters and brother might have felt the same way too. I don't know for sure if they did, because I never asked them.

After spending a few days and sleeping on the couch at night, it would be time for Mr. Joyce to leave. I did not like saying goodbye to the plump, balding man with the wide smile.

In another year or so, he'd be back—I hoped.

Many smiles left the house when he drove off laughing and waving as we all stood by the road waving back to him.

It was hard to go back into the house after we saw him turn onto Stump Road and disappear.

Mr. Joyce did come back several times. The extra smiles and laughter returned with him and faded when he left as quickly as Mom's and Dad's cigarette smoke disappeared in a breeze. At least the good memories stuck around.

More on John

John finally got to be almost healthy. I say "almost" because he always caught whatever bug was going around. I still kept an eye on him, but I didn't worry about him as much as I did before.

He was a skinny kid and could move very quickly once the casts were off for good. The corrective shoes slowed him down when he had to wear them. They were nothing more than shoes worn on the wrong feet. They helped his feet keep from turning in.

Special shoe stores probably had shoes made for kids with John's problem, but Dad couldn't afford to buy them even if the shoe stores did carry them.

I tried wearing my own shoes on the opposite feet. It hurt too much to wear them that way for very long.

I admired John because he just ignored them and didn't complain when Mom put them on him.

First Grade

I was completely put into shock when I started first grade. I had Miss MacKaig. She made Grandma Simpson look like a young woman. She was short and thin as a rail. Her hair was always in a bun. It was so tightly bound that I swore that I could hear hairs popping out of the front of her head when school started in the morning. As the day wore on, the bun would loosen up a little. It's a good thing it did loosen because I think the pain from her hair constantly on the edge of being pulled out by the roots, added to her mean disposition.

I got on her nerves a lot. I didn't have the sense to look like I was paying attention like the rest of the class. My eyes would wander to the window to see what the other classes were doing during their playtime or what I'd be able to do in gym class that afternoon. She'd be at my desk quicker than I could get my eyes and mind back on what was happening in class. She must have studied the sneak attack on Pearl Harbor that Dad talked about.

A few times she put me in the corner behind the upright piano that came with every classroom. She'd pull it out from the corner just enough to get me squeezed in and put the piano back in place quickly so I wouldn't escape. One time after shoving me back there, she sat down and played the piano and had the rest of the class sing. I had to put my hands over my ears because the racket was just too much.

I sure wished that she had taken more piano lessons before she became a teacher. I also promised myself to pay better attention in class. The promise I made didn't last very long before I broke it.

If I hadn't pestered her too much, she'd just have me sit in the corner facing the wall with a dunce hat on my head for what seemed like a few hours. If I got her dander only half up, she'd place me under the center of her desk, sit down, and compact me into the front board that was put there for modesty reasons.

I found out why the board was really there: The board was made from thick, strong wood to keep kids like me from being pushed through. She had hard, bony knees and used them to squash me against the board.

First Communion

The early spring brought something to take time away from listening to the kids' shows on Saturday morning: First Communion classes started at St. Bridget's. The class always began at nine.

I was now old enough to walk to church by myself. I only had to walk up our street, go down Stump Road, cross the bridge over Skaneateles Creek, climb up the trail that went over the railroad tracks, walk over Jordan Road, and I was there. It took maybe three minutes.

When the class was done, I'd run like the dickens to get home. The Saturday morning kids' shows on the radio had already started, and I didn't want to miss any more of a show than I had to.

The nun who taught the class was formed by God to look like an out-of-round bowling ball. She never turned her head to either side by moving it with her neck. I wondered if she even had one. I couldn't tell because the black and white uniform she wore covered all of her except her face, hands, and her black-shoed feet.

We all made sure that we had our catechisms with us because Sister possessed the third hand of God—a strong ruler that she occasionally used as a pointer. Over the years, she had changed it from being a pointer into a poorly disguised weapon. Sister would use it as a pointer once in a while just to throw us off guard. I feared it. It didn't take long for me to have the fear turn into a real thing.

She would have us repeat certain prayers over and over again. Some prayers were even in Latin.

I asked Dad about Latin. He told me that he had studied it in school and it was a dead language. I figured what he said was right because dead things can haunt people, and we were surely being haunted.

I'd get into trouble when I hesitated on the "Hail Mary." I'd get to the part about the "fruit of thy womb" and wonder how fruit could be in a womb and what a womb was. This would cause me to stop to think about it. If some other helpless child had already stumbled on a prayer, her anger would be almost at the boiling point when I hesitated, and I would become the Saturday Example. The ruler would change into a painful weapon as it gave my outstretched hand a painful rap across the knuckles.

We were all terrified of the holy lady. After all, she was close to being a sister of God Himself. God's wrath was unthinkable. How would He act when He learned that an almost sister to Him was being tormented by me?

My overactive mind didn't even venture to the answer to that question because I had witnessed what an almost-sister of God could do.

I became a firm believer in the Wrath of God.

One time she came after me when I was behaving—it was a rare thing. When she was coming toward me, I shouted out, "It wasn't me who was talking!"

I was willing to take the pill of the ruler when I did something wrong or forgot a part of a prayer, but this was too much. The anger that had been building up in me exploded. She could see the look of complete hatred directed right at her as she told me to put my hand out.

On the way home I knew that I was in for it. I had committed a major sin by talking out. I knew that the Wrath of God in the human form of my mother would be coming to the surface soon.

I wasn't home five minutes when Sister pulled up out front in the black nun sedan. I watched from the living room window as she got out, closed the car door carefully, and glided up the walk to our house like a ghost sliding across ice.

Mom heard her knock at the door and let her in. I heard Sister tell Mom what had happened in class. She also hinted to Mom about my upbringing.

After she effortlessly glided back to the car and left, Mom told me that what I had done was very bad, pulled down my pants, put me across her knee, and gave me a sound spanking.

I wailed like a banshee and couldn't sit down for a long time.

Terry and Pat went upstairs before the spanking started to get themselves out of sight. They didn't want to watch. Besides, maybe they'd be next.

I put my mind to learning the prayers and the correct way of receiving communion at the top of my list. I made sure I did the right moves when Sister used her clicker during the last two Saturday lessons.

I was allowed to receive my First Communion with the rest of the class after going to my First Confession. I didn't mention anything about the problem with Sister. After all, Father Mc-Mahon was closer to God than Mom, and she had put a serious hurting on me for what I had done. The wrath of a priest must be close to the Wrath of God.

The wrath of Mom was as close to it as I wanted to get. I had my First Communion under sin and it bothered me.

First Grade Ends

With notes being sent home causing Mom great upset that often led to a sore bottom, Grandma Simpson moving in the opening month of the school year, and Dad hitting the bottle, it wasn't a very good year at school.

I had to sweat out Mom opening up the yearly report card. I'd passed again! How?

Miss MacKaig wasn't the only first grade teacher. The other one was my Aunt Pat. I knew Miss MacKaig didn't want to have me placed in Aunt Pat's class because she probably felt sorry for her. After all, didn't Aunt Pat already have to see me enough by living so close to our house?

I was starting to catch on to why I was passing without doing a heck of a lot to improve my learning skills. I was beginning to do well in school reasoning. At least I was learning something.

Summertime 1953

For some reason, I remember the summer after getting through first grade as being very hot. Terry, Pat, John, and I would have great fun running under the hose water. One of us would hold it and the others would go screaming through the water. We'd attach the metal water sprinkler, take turns running through it, or see who could stand right over it the longest. I'd will myself to stay over it the longest.

The hot days brought hot nights. The roof would bake all day and hold the heat for most of the night. Mom would let us stay up a little later on very hot nights to give the house a chance to cool off a bit.

We didn't have a fan in the house because one would cost too much.

When she thought we'd survive up there without baking, the nightly routine would begin. We'd all take turns washing our hands and faces and brushing our teeth. Next, if Dad didn't have a part-time job and was home from work, we'd kiss and hug him good night and climb up the stairs. Mom would follow us up and we'd all say our nightly prayers together. First would come the God bless so and so followed by "Now I Lay Me Down to Sleep." After prayers were said, Mom would come to each of us and give us a kiss and hug.

I liked this time of the day.

It was hard to get to sleep even if we were over-tired. If there wasn't a breeze blowing through the windows, we'd lay there slowly roasting to death whispering to each other across the room. When we got too loud, Mom would yell up to us to settle down. After a pause, we'd begin to whisper again. I think Pat would fall asleep first. Soon after Pat conked out, Terry would go silent. Then I'd nod off.

I felt closer to my sisters during these moments because we were all doing something Mom had told us not to do.

It was very hard for Patty to do something wrong and work with Terry and me as a team.

Grandma Simpson Goes to Church

On a warm Sunday morning after we went to church, Dad and I drove Grandma Simpson up to Skaneateles so she could go to St. James Episcopal Church. Dad had to visit someone, so he told me to wait for Grandma.

Thayer Park is right next to the church and has green wooden benches to sit on. I sat there watching the sailboats and

Chris Craft boats go by. I loved the sound of the deep-throated powerboats and the huge waves they'd toss aside.

Grandma's church service was a good half-hour longer than the ones we went to every Sunday at St. Bridget's Church in Skaneateles Falls. But the time went by quickly as I watched the boats go by.

Out of the corner of my eye, I noticed people coming out of the church, so I went up to the door to meet her. She introduced me to the minister and I used proper manners. Manners were very important to Mom and Grandma.

Grandma and I then walked across the street. As we walked by the library, Skaneateles Savings Bank, and the Masonic Temple, I made sure I stayed to the road side of her like Mom had taught me.

When we got in front of Riddler's newsstand and soda fountain store, she told me to wait while she went inside.

To my great surprise, she walked out with two ice cream cones. Was she going to eat both of them? She handed one to me. I was almost too dumbstruck to say thank you.

We had no sooner taken a few paces when she tripped over a step that jutted out into the sidewalk.

I stood there with my mouth open and froze as a man ran over and quickly helped her up.

The damage had been done. She had dropped her ice cream, torn a stocking, and scratched her knee. She acted embarrassed about falling in front of so many people. The special time I briefly had with Grandma melted like the dropped ice cream on the sidewalk.

I didn't know what to say, so I kept my mouth shut.

It was a very silent walk back to Dad's car. I kept myself busy looking out the car window all the way back home. She didn't say anything to Dad about what had happened.

I felt sorry for Grandma and guilty that I didn't help her up.

I just didn't know what to do with my ice cream cone when she fell!

Dad gets a Second Job

We didn't see much of Dad all fall because he got an extra job to try to make "the ends meet." He worked for Mr. Larabee in Mottville. He had a toy factory that made wooden train sets and tracks for the trains to ride on.

The wonderful smell of maple sawdust would still be on Dad's work clothes the next morning when we got up to go to school. It made me feel sad to see him go off to his regular job looking so tired.

Dad called a worker for the State "a feeder at the public trough." The trough didn't have much feed in it, but we never went to bed totally hungry either.

The Five-Day Vacation Theory, Part III

Just before Thanksgiving time, Mom started wearing baggy shirts again and putting on weight. We would be tied with the Tambroni family.

My sisters and I were all excited and couldn't wait to tell the Tambroni kids when we got on the bus.

Mom wasn't thrilled about it at all. Maybe she was getting tired of her five-day vacations at the same place. I started to get worried about her.

Thanksgiving 1953

Mom would bake pies on the Wednesday before Thanksgiving for the big dinner at Grandma's and Grandpa's house.

She'd give me a piece of raw dough to chew on. The smells were so grand and gave a hint of the soon to come best meal of the year.

On Thanksgiving Day in the late morning, the whole family got dressed in our Sunday best.

Dad would carry the pies, Mom would carry John, and the rest of us would follow. Entering our grandparents' house was a treat in itself. The smells that waved over us were enough to make me drool like a dog. We'd go in, say our polite greetings, and talk.

I liked to get under foot in the kitchen. Aunt Mary would be nice to me for a change and use a gentle hip or knee to push me out of the way. (Her usual hip move would send me flying and the knee bend into my thigh would hurt.) If I were quick enough, I'd snitch a piece of candy from a bowl to keep the sounds in my stomach down to a dull roar. I'd keep one eye on Aunt Mary and the other on the candy bowl. It was my self-assigned duty in the kitchen to eat as much of the candy as I could, without Aunt Mary catching me in the act, until the big feast was ready to eat.

Uncle Danny, Aunt Pat, John, and Mary Kay would be there too. It would be a very crowded house.

While the feast was being prepared, Uncle Danny sometimes would be at the kitchen table slowly lifting a spoon of tea an inch or two above the cup and dropping it back in. He did this to cool the tea. I thought it was a neat trick because he'd do it without spilling a drop on the saucer as he talked, told jokes, and laughed. All the while he'd be looking around the room and not even glancing at the cup.

The day was filled with laughter, "remember when's," and clanking silverware.

When the table was set and the food ready, Grandma Quigley would be wheeled in and placed at one end of the table and Grandpa Quigley would be at the other end.

The adults would sit at the dining room table and the rest of us would eat at a small table set up in the living room.

Aunt Ann liked to sit and eat with us. She would help the little ones get their food into their mouths without making too much of a mess.

We all ate as if food was never going to be seen in the house again. It was painful to finally get up, but we somehow always had room to sit down an hour or so later to finish off Mom's wonderful apple, cherry, and pumpkin pies.

We "young-uns" never got into trouble after the feast because we were too full to move. It was a happy day made even more special by Aunt Mary becoming a nice person for a short while.

We didn't walk home after the big meal—We waddled at a very slow pace.

Where was Grandma Simpson on Thanksgiving Day? I knew she had some friends from England living in the area, but I didn't know their names or where they lived. I think she went to visit them.

Christmas 1953

The Christmas season was my favorite time of the year. Right around Thanksgiving, I'd start to think about what I wanted Santa to bring me. I knew the "naughty or nice" thing was correct because he seldom left much for me. It was hard to understand why Pat didn't get much because she was always so good. Maybe Santa got her confused with some other girl named Pat who was more like me and also lived somewhere in the area.

I kept what I wanted to the bare minimum to keep the disappointment down.

We children all would write what we wanted on a piece of paper. Mom or Dad would open up the stove door, and we'd throw our papers into the hot fire.

Mom said that the paper would burn, turn to smoke, float up into the sky, and turn back into paper. The wind would then carry the paper to the North Pole.

Mom said it was true, so it had to be.

Our way of getting our lists to Santa was even more amazing to me than the belly button method of babies coming into the world.

Mom often said, "Ignorance is bliss." She was right.

We'd go to bed on Christmas Eve all excited. Once we got settled in, I'd start to get scared. I'd listen for Santa to come, hoping that he didn't climb up the stairs to check on us. I'd fall asleep thinking about him.

The next morning came way too early for Mom and Dad. We'd get them up so we could get downstairs to see what the scary man had left for us.

To my wide-eyed amazement, he had left me a beautiful Marx electric train set. All my brothers and sisters also got what they had asked Santa to bring.

It was an unbelievable day. I spent most of it setting up the train and playing with it. Dad helped me, and we had a good time together.

I kept thinking about Santa and how he could have possibly known that I was dying to have a train set. I had told only Mom and Dad about it.

Any doubts about believing in Santa and what some kids had said about him in school and on the bus vanished. I now believed in Santa with all my heart and soul.

But again, maybe he had confused me with another Mike in the area.

What did that Mike get?

Mom always cooked a turkey dinner complete with all the trimmings for us on Christmas. The smells coming from the kitchen would drive us all to distraction. The turkey always took longer to cook in the brown paper bag because Mom would have to fight with the old gas stove for the four hours or so that it took to cook.

Once I caught Mom looking at the stove and talking to it. She said a bad word and was a little embarrassed that I had heard her. I couldn't find fault with her because the words I had been directing towards the stove were much worse than what she had said.

It's a good thing that Mom didn't know what I was saying in my head. Many times before she had shocked me by saying, "Michael, I know what you're thinking. Stop it right now."

We finally all sat down in the small kitchen to eat the feast. It was very crowded around the table. Dad said the blessing and we all chimed in except for Grandma Simpson. She just bowed her head and said her own silent prayer.

We all went to bed that night with big smiles on our faces. It was a grand day.

The Railroad

The Skaneateles Short Line Railroad Company was running small steam locomotives. We couldn't see them going back and forth from Skaneateles to Hartlot from our house, but we could hear them and see their smoke rising above the Welch Allyn factory across the creek from us.

The track ran in front of St. Bridget's Church and right along the side of Jordan Road.

On a cold Sunday morning when we came out of church, we saw one of the locomotives still breathing but stopped just before the Waterbury Felt Company. Many men were working around her.

Dad told Mom to go on home with the little ones. Dad led me up the road to see what was going on. The engine had jumped the tracks.

I watched very closely as the men used huge jacks and levers to get it back on the tracks. The engine sat there breathing very slowly and with what seemed like patience as the men worked. It didn't take them very long to finish the job.

The engineer and the stoker climbed up into the cab. In no time, the engine was breathing at a faster pace. It backed very slowly away from the damaged track and retreated to the engine yard in Skaneateles where it could rest until the track was repaired.

The train shouldn't have to work on Sunday anyway.

Where the train's wheels had run aground on the railroad ties showed me just how much even a small engine weighed. Several of the ties were indented at least two inches, and the ones that had rotted some were broken into two pieces as if they had been cut with a very dull knife.

I had longed to ride in the cab of one of the steamers. When I was near the tracks when one came by, I'd wave to the engineer hoping to see it slow down, stop, and pick me up. The engineers always waved, but the steamers never slowed.

The timetable was set, and I was not included as one of their stops.

It wasn't many years after when I suddenly noticed that the familiar sound of the steamers was missing. I was so used to their breathing in the background that I took them for granted.

I had been hearing a low hum but figured it was some new machine in Welch Allyn making the noise. My mind had only gotten to the point of figuring it must be a huge machine that didn't run all the time.

Mom told me that the steamers had been retired and replaced by a blue diesel engine. The new sound I had been hearing wasn't in Welch Allyn.

I was in shock. I never thought that the steamers would be torn out of my life. I don't know how I could have studied them more as they had passed, but I wished I had. Was life like that? I was confused and upset.

I saw the new blue diesel shortly after Mom told me about it. It looked the same in the front and in the back. I couldn't even tell which end was which. The engineer would just stand up and move to the other seat when the train changed directions. When I waved to the engineer, he didn't lift his arm as high as he did before, and he didn't smile at me in the same way either.

I couldn't blame him. I felt sad too.

The McEnenys

John McEneny spent lots of time in his garden. He'd work slowly because of his age and would often rest himself by leaning on his hoe handle. I think Dad learned how to grow a good garden and take care of it from him when he was a boy. The potato plants were Mr. McEneny's favorites. He'd weed with extra care around them and made sure that they all were hilled properly. There never would be a potato famine in Stump City as long as he and Dad were growing them.

Mr. McEneny often asked me, "Have you seen the pony?" If he was in his metal outdoor chair that he kept parked by the ancient lilac bush, he'd point to the little barn at the edge of his property next to Mame Wickham's place as he said it. I'd look over there and not see a thing. He had shown me the inside of the little barn many times. It looked too small to hold a pony, and there was no sign that a horse had ever been inside.

I never did see the pony and neither did any of my brothers and sisters.

Mrs. McEneny would often offer me a drink of iced tea and a cookie. She was even shorter than Aunt Ann. Her energy level was as high as Aunt Mary's, but she didn't act like her. She didn't sit still much and kept herself busy in and out of the house. She was a no-nonsense type of lady, but she had a very warm heart.

I loved Helen and John McEneny.

The only time Mr. McEneny got mad at me was when I walked up the sidewalk that ran along the side of the house and led to the back kitchen door. The living room was right next to the sidewalk and the window was open. He was listening to a beloved Yankee game on the radio. I think I yelled to Terry to wait for me. Apparently I broke his mental vision of what was happening on the playing field.

He yelled, "?&^%#, be quiet out there!"

I had never heard him swear before and it startled me. I turned around and went back home. I was too afraid to go in.

Their daughter, Rose, was a bundle of laughing, joking energy. She was a cheerleader in school and thought it her job to continue cheering others on long after the game was over. Her bedroom was as big as the one all of us kids slept in. She had it decorated with pictures and banners. Rose often had friends over to her house. The place would appear to be laughing and moving from side to side when she did. The only time she and her friends were quiet was when her dad was listening to a game.

If Grandma Simpson was out trying to hasten the exit of

another old lady, Rose would baby-sit for us when Mom and Dad went out.

Our house seemed to start bubbling as soon as Rose came through the door. If I started to get a little rowdy, all she had to do to calm me down and get me back on track, was give me a certain look as she placed a hand on one of her hips. The silent message quickly registered in my head.

She was loads of fun but didn't put up with any nonsense from me. It didn't take long for me to learn where the line was, and I didn't cross it very often with her. I wanted Rose to like me.

More on Grandpa Quigley

Grandpa Quigley retired from Waterbury Felt Company just before Thanksgiving. He was sixty-six and the work was wearing him out. He had worked hard all of his life and needed to rest.

I think he would have liked to go back to the Quigley Bog in Northern Ireland for one last time, but Grandma wouldn't hold up on the long trip, and there just wasn't enough money to do it anyway. He spent his time puttering in the garden and, when he could catch a ride, going to Murray's Bar for a pint or two.

One day he got really sick. Dr. Horne came from Skaneateles to the house to check him over and immediately drove Grandpa to the hospital. Grandpa had had a heart attack and had to stay in there for several days.

Dad and I went to visit Grandpa. He looked pale and weak, but wanted to go home. After he had stayed a week in the hospital, the doctor let him escape and go back home.

I don't think he missed Grandma as much as he did his chewing tobacco.

He became content just to sit in his chair in the living room, chew tobacco, and listen to the radio.

If Dad and I were visiting and the radio was off, I'd sit on the floor in front of Grandpa and listen to him tell stories about ancient relatives, the Old Country, and the hated English invaders.

He wouldn't remember that I was half English. Even if he did, he would have said the things he said about them anyway.

Grandpa would often put a new wad of chewing tobacco in his mouth before he'd start telling me a long story. The same shiny brass spittoon I had put my hands into as soon as I could crawl, was always on the floor on the right side of his well-worn, stuffed chair. He was a right-headed spitter and hit the center of the spittoon most of the time.

Aunt Mary always had newspaper under it to catch any missed shots.

When he was ready to take a shot, he'd use his left arm and push on the arm rest of the chair, move his weight to his right hip, bend his now-slanted back, and let the juice go. If he made a perfect shot and Aunt Ann had emptied the spittoon, it would make a pinging sound and echo just a bit. His actions were now slower than I remembered, but they were still smooth.

With over forty years of chewing under his belt, the whole thing was done without any thought. He had all the moves down like professional dancers going around a ballroom floor.

Foot Stool Willy

The most fascinating story Grandpa told was about his great-uncle Willy. Willy read about the gold rush in California and decided he would go try his luck. He scraped enough money together to buy a ticket on a ship headed to New York City. From there he traveled by train as far west as it would take him and joined up with some gang of men who were headed for California.

Grandpa never mentioned how long it took Willy to reach California.

When Willy got there, he bought a shovel, pickaxe, some food, and went into the back country to search for gold.

Most of the men who searched never found enough to even pay for their equipment, but his great-uncle Willy got lucky and found lots of it. His claim wasn't the Mother Lode, whatever that means, but he was able to sell it to some mining company for what to him was a small fortune.

Willy got himself a ticket to New York City on a Yankee Clipper. As soon as he got to New York City, he found a ship sailing for Ireland and bought passage.

The whole adventure lasted a little more than a year.

When he got back home, Willy got a nice little cottage, sat in a chair with a bottle of good Irish whiskey, and put his feet up on a stool. He didn't work a lick for the rest of his life.

His neighbors gave him the nickname "Foot Stool Willy", and it stuck for the rest of his life.

Great-uncle Willy told Grandpa that he should never go to America. He said, "The country is too long and too wide and a man would just get lost in it."

After he finished the story, I thought that maybe Grandpa had sat in front of Foot Stool Willy so many years and miles ago just as I was sitting in front of Grandpa then.

I got to know Grandpa pretty well just sitting in front of him and listening. As a boy, he must have kept his mouth shut just like me while ancient relatives told him stories.

Grandpa didn't take to heart what Foot Stool Willy had told him because he came here with his brothers and sisters around 1908. His father, Patrick Quigley, wasn't going to come, but there would be no family left behind to stay with him if he remained in Ireland.

Grandpa said that he had to get his brothers and sisters out of Ireland because they would have starved to death if he hadn't.

Things in Ireland must have been really bad.

Grandpa thought that America was as close to Heaven as he'd get until he died.

Grandpa would often say to me, "Gosh and begora, Michael me boy, 'tis a fine grand country!"

Second Grade

I can't remember much about second grade, but I know I had a beautiful teacher, Mrs. Robedee. I immediately fell in love with her. She was not beautiful in the physical sense. She was beautiful in mind and spirit. She was soft-spoken, a bit shy, and very calm. If I wasn't paying attention, she'd gently remind me to stay with the class.

Maybe she had talked to my past two teachers, and they had come up with a new plan of attack. Mrs. Robedee probably got laughed at when she suggested being less stern with me.

Anyway, it worked and it might have lengthened her stay as a teacher for so many years after, because kids like me behaved better in her class than they did in most other teachers' classes.

She had the gift of survival.

I was a very good boy in her class, and my grades were much better than they had been the first two years. I didn't want to disappoint her in any way and found it pretty easy to keep my nose clean.

I was learning about both the good and bad powers of women. She had me wrapped around her little finger. She was like an older Terry.

I didn't have to worry about carrying my report card home. It was a nice feeling. I knew I wouldn't have her again as a teacher, but at least I'd be able to say hello to her in the hall.

It must have annoyed both Miss MacKaig and Mrs. Peak to have a young teacher show them up. That gave me a good feeling and made me smile at the thought of it.

Chris

Toward the middle of August, Mom left for another five-day vacation. Dad picked up her bag of vacation clothes and they left. Mom was walking very slowly down the walk to the car with Dad holding onto her arm. He seemed to be very concerned about her. I was worried.

Dad took us all in the old sedan to see our new brother, Chris, and Mom in the hospital. We looked at him for the first time. His blond hair was like Patty's. He was much bigger than the other babies, and he was by far the champion crier in the crowded nursery. It made me wonder about the noise level in the house when he got home.

Terry looked at Chris in a different way. I knew she was thinking about diapers and hoping she was still too young to change them. I felt sorry for her because I had seen some real bad explosions when Mom had opened up the packages of goods. I didn't stick around long, but Terry had to watch to see how Mom took off the diaper, cleaned up the baby of the moment, and put a clean diaper on.

The only other job that could possibly be worse was cleaning out the outhouse.

I don't ever remember not seeing diapers hanging on the line to dry.

Next, we went to see Mom. She wasn't her normal self. Oh, she was glad to see us and gave us all big hugs, but she had to make an effort to stay focused. She just wasn't acting like Mom.

While Mom was in the hospital, Aunt Ann wasn't taking care of us. Grandma Simpson didn't have a job helping some old lady leave this earth, so she took charge. She ran the house in the way she thought it should be run.

I stayed outside a lot and played on the porch when it was raining. Terry was old enough to help her out. Pat, Mom's Little Helper, did what she could to help, which was a lot considering her age.

Pat was rewarded for her help with extra penny candies. Terry didn't get any and didn't expect to, either.

It was John's turn to be thrown out and venture into the bedroom with us. He wanted to be with us, so the change wasn't a bad time for him.

Another used bed was found from a neighbor, and Dad put it just down the wall from mine. With four beds and two dressers in the room, it was getting a bit cramped in there.

Mom seemed to be going through the motions when she got home. Her heart wasn't in it. I remember her trying to feed Chris in the living room. She was always relaxed when she was feeding one of my sisters or John. She'd talk to us if we were in the house. Now I could see real pain on her face when she fed Chris. When she was done, Chris would continue to cry. I didn't think he was getting enough to drink.

Chris had to have formula, and Mom became even more unlike herself.

It wasn't long after that when Dad told us that he had to take Mom to the hospital. When he got back, he told us that Mom's nerves were shot and she needed a long rest.

The house wasn't the same without Mom around to keep things in their proper order. Grandma Simpson sure wasn't at all like Mom—The only way they were the same was the way they talked with an English accent.

Come to think of it, Mom wasn't Mom either.

I don't remember how long Mom was in the hospital, but I know it felt like a long time.

Just before Dad went to pick her up at the hospital, he told us to be extra good and help Mom out as much as we could.

She was almost her old self again in the way she moved, acted, and spoke to us.

Those of us who were old enough became much better helpers to lighten Mom's huge work load. Dad also did much more around the house and even stayed away from The Drink for a long time.

We were all so happy to have her home.

Pirates!

On one cool summer day, I took it into my head to go look for treasure. I had heard a story about Black Beard the Pirate or some such on the radio, and I wanted to see if I could find a treasure chest. I first had to figure out a spot to dig.

With several years of logic and reasoning under my belt, I came to the conclusion that along the edge of our road would be the perfect spot. After all, it was away from the creek and next to a road that the pirates might use to carry a treasure chest. Wouldn't it be much easier than blazing their own trail?

I went to Dad's tool shed and got his shovel and walked on the road to the front of the McEneny house. Right across the street from their house were the overgrown ruins of the button factory. What a perfect spot for a pirate's treasure chest to be buried!

I started digging a hole no more than five feet from the edge of the road. I dug for at least an hour and hadn't found anything. Tired and a bit discouraged, I rested on my shovel the way Mr. McEneny and Dad would. I had just started to dig some more when Mom called me in for lunch. I stuck the shovel in the deep hole and went in to eat.

With a full stomach and aching hands, I went out to dig again. I had been digging no more than ten minutes when I saw a shiny object in the hole. I bent down and picked it up. It was a worn fifty-cent piece! My jaw flew open and my eyes got big. I shoveled like a madman for at least another half-hour and found another fifty-cent piece. My heart was pounding in my chest. I dug, for I don't know how much longer, and decided that I had found all the treasure. Totally pooped out, I slowly filled the hole back in.

I hadn't looked up from my work during the whole time.

When I turned to go back home and tell Mom the wonderful news, I noticed that Mr. McEneny was sitting in his chair by the lilac bush watching me. He waved me to come up to him.

He said, "Michael, I've been spying you, I have. What have you been doing?"

I told him what I had been digging for and showed him what I had found.

He said, "Gosh and begora. 'T'is a small treasure you've found, indeed."

I agreed with him and asked permission to go tell Mom.

He waved the back of his hand in my direction and said, "Be gone with you."

I was so happy that Mr. McEneny could share the joy of my good fortune.

I ran back home dragging the shovel behind me in one hand and tightly holding onto the treasure in the other.

Mom was amazed when I told her the story of my find, and how I decided to dig the hole where I did. She kept turning the fifty-cent pieces over and over in her hand. I could tell she was thinking real hard. She finally stopped her deep thinking, gave them back to me, and smiled as she looked out the window that faced the McEneny home.

My allowance was five cents a week. At the time, five cents would buy me a full sized candy bar at Cronaeur's General Store. By using logic and reasoning, I had found a whole dollar. What would it buy at Cronaeur's?

I wondered if Foot Stool Willy had felt the same way I did when he found gold.

Mowing—Part I

Mom loved to work outside in her flower gardens and to mow the lawn. She said that it "blew the stink off".

She might have meant the continuous smell of baby diapers over the years that had taken up housekeeping in her nose.

Mom would get the hand-powered reel mower out of the tool shed and attack the lawn. She would fly back and forth in a big hurry. If clothes were on the line, she'd duck under them without easing up her pace. Often, she'd forget to take off the apron that she wore all the time when she was in the house. The stress lines on her face would slowly fade away. By the time she was done, she'd be in a slight lather. I'd get her a glass of water and we'd sit down on the back ledge and talk.

It was a relaxing time for her.

I tried to push the mower, but it was hard for me to do. It took me much longer to go back and forth than it took her. She'd stand there giving me encouragement and smiled when I stopped.

I think that she was thankful that I couldn't mow the lawn yet. She wanted an excuse to get outside without feeling guilty about something she should be doing inside.

She was a very hard, fast worker and would only sit down to rest when the two youngest at the time went down for their afternoon naps.

The Laundry

Mom had an old Maytag washing machine in the basement. In the summer heat, it was nice to be down there with her when she did the laundry. In the winter, it would be very cold down there and she would have to wear a coat.

She'd fill the machine and big rinsing tub with water from a hose, add detergent to the machine after she had turned it on, and begin the washing. The dark clothes would go in first. The washer would do its job for about ten minutes and she'd turn it off. Next she'd run all the clothes through the hand-crank wringer and the clothes would drop into the rinsing tub. She'd swish the clothes around in the tub by hand for several minutes and then run them through the wringer into a basket. When she was done with the dark clothes, she'd empty the washer and rinse tub into the drain and start all over again.

While the second load of washing was being punished by the old Maytag, Mom would go outside and hang the clothes on the line. When they were hung, it was back to the basement for the second load.

In the wintertime, she'd bring in frozen clothes from the line and put them on drying racks around the stove to finish the task. It was hard work for her.

When Mom thought I was old enough, she would let me turn the wringer while she fed the clothes through it. Once she got her finger in it and let out a yell. I backed the wringer off her finger and watched her do a strange jig around the dirt basement floor.

It was hard to keep from laughing, but the thought of a swat across the bottom helped me hold it in.

It must have been even harder for Mom not to swear as she danced.

Dad was the only one allowed to wear a shirt for just one day. The rest of us, including Mom, would wear the same clothes for several days before they were washed. We were always told to stay clean. It helped cut down on the amount of washing she had to do.

Mom would do a super job of ironing Dad's dress clothes for work and the dress clothes we wore on Sundays or special events. The rest of the clothes were done well enough to keep us looking neat for school.

Hand-me-downs

It was rare for any of us to get new clothes. Most of what we wore came from the Walton and the Tambroni families. The Waltons had more children than our family did, and many of them older than we were. Once all of them outgrew what the older ones had worn, the well-worn, faded clothes would come to our house in paper bags. The Tambroni family had the same number of children as we did but they were smaller. Mom, Mrs. Walton, and Mrs. Tambroni would exchange clothes like stocks in New York. Once we were done with the clothes, they would be shipped out to another family.

There was a family with less than ours somewhere in the community? Amazing!

During a long break between exchanging hand-me-downs, Mom would buy iron-on knee patches and leg pant extenders at Talbot's Store in Skaneateles. It wasn't too embarrassing to wear the pants because a few other kids in class had the same extenders and patches on their pants. We weren't the only family in the area living low on the hog.

Rich

If I felt bad about wearing the pants, I would be reminded every day that there were kids far worse off. The daily reminder came when the bus stopped in Hartlot to pick up kids from a huge run-down house with broken windows and holes in the roof.

I think there were more kids living in this house than there were in the Walton family, but they lived too far away to be in the contest for the most kids.

Their clothes were tattered, torn, and soiled. In the cold winters most of them didn't even have jackets. It would take them half the school day to get warmed up.

It's a good thing they went to school because if they weren't thawed out in the day, they probably would have frozen to death during the night.

I made a habit of counting heads when they got on the bus with the temperature around the zero mark. I was worried that one of them might die during the night.

I don't know how they kept warm over the weekends or on days when the temperature was around zero. School would be closed because it was too cold for the kids to walk to school or wait for a bus.

One of them, Rich, was in my class. Nobody wanted to sit next to any of them because they had an off smell.

One day, because Pete was skipping school again or had to do some work for his father, Rich sat next to me. For some reason, I said hello to him. He mumbled some greeting and we started talking. The more he talked, the more I liked him. He would sit next to me from then on if Pete wasn't in school, which was at least once a week. We became good friends and played together during recess.

He came over to our house a few times. Mom always had a huge snack ready for us. It was much bigger than a usual snack. Rich would thank Mom more than once while he and I were eating.

I figured out what Mom was doing the first time she put out the snack. All she had to do was look at him to know that he was "Lacking."

The Tambroni Family

The Tambroni family lived across the creek and just down the road from Welch Allyn. Mrs. Tambroni was also a war bride and from England. She and Mom were close and often she and her family would be at our house, or we'd walk to their house.

Mrs. Tambroni spoke with a weird accent because she was raised close to London.

When I was younger, I didn't know that Mom had an accent too, until after several people asked her where she was born in England, or would say, "What a beautiful accent!"

Mom said that she took pride in proper grammar and the good use of "The King's Language."

I always thought that people stopped their talking to listen to her because of her strong presence. I was half right about that.

Anyway, Mrs. Tambroni and Mom were both in competition to see who could have the most children. At the moment, they were tied, but Mrs. Tambroni would be going in for a five-day vacation pretty soon because she was wearing a baggy shirt and had a huge belly.

One Sunday afternoon the whole Tambroni tribe climbed into the family sedan and came over for a visit. Mr. Tambroni was a nice, excitable Italian man and used the word "gumba" like the rest of us use the word "the." We were all outside talking and playing as we usually did. All of a sudden, Mrs. Tambroni let out an ear-splitting scream and waddled as quickly as she could towards the sedan. Mr. Tambroni and Dad quickly overtook her.

The sedan was slowly but surely gaining speed as it rolled backward down the driveway, crossed the road, and headed toward the dirt pathway that went to the base of the dam.

I saw the top of a head. It was little Steve Tambroni. He was sitting in the front seat holding onto the steering wheel with both hands in a death grip. The car was now gaining speed and heading for the sharp bend that led down to the dam.

Just before it got to the steep drop-off above the creek, Dad caught up to the sedan, opened the door, and pulled on the emergency brake.

When Mr. Tambroni got to the car, I could see him waving his hands and arms in ways that are not humanly possible. I could faintly hear Italian words coming from his lips. I could tell he was swearing because some of the words had a familiar ring to them. He yanked poor little Steve out of the car, swatted his butt, and drove the car back up the hill.

Steve had already run back to his Mom and into her arms. She held him as close to her as she could in her condition, and they both cried.

Little Steve's driving days were over.

The word spread quickly around Stump City about what had happened. All of us thought Dad was a hero. It was a wonderful feeling to have a hero for a dad.

More on Terry

Terry always liked animals. She had trained our dog, Prince, to do many tricks. The dog would follow her around and kept an eye on her all the time. I liked Prince too, but not the way Terry did. She would brush the dog while he patiently sat still. His coat was always nice, unless he had rolled in a dead woodchuck. He wouldn't smell bad for long. Terry would place him in the same old tub we use to take baths and get him cleaned up as good as new. They were a good team.

Meet the Rooster

Dad brought home a huge old rooster he got on a whim from Pete the Peddler. It was the same one I'd noticed a few weeks earlier because he had very strange, scary eyes. I think his look made the women, who were looking for an expensive meal, decide on another less threatening victim.

I don't know why Dad did this because roosters don't lay eggs. I learned that years ago from Uncle Jimmy, and I know Uncle Jimmy had learned that from Dad. Dad probably got it at a discount price just like Mom got fruit that wouldn't last much longer at a lower price.

The rooster's home was an old doghouse. Terry took an interest in the feathered beast and would feed and water him. He always examined me up and down like I was a giant piece of corn. It scared me.

He and Prince didn't quite see eye-to-eye. Prince would stay out of the rooster's way and avoid what the red-feathered creature thought was his territory. See, Prince had learned very early on that the rooster had a sharp beak and the feathered beast wasn't at all afraid of him or anything else for that matter.

I thought Prince had the right idea and I did the same. The only exception I made was throwing dirt clods his way to watch him attack them. If I came close to his country, I made sure not to cross his border. I'm sure he'd go after me like he went after the dirt clods.

More on Grandma Simpson

Grandma Simpson started a job with another old lady right after Mom got home from the hospital. She would be trying her best again to complete her business of seeing another old lady go to the other side. So far she had a perfect record, except for the one time when she came home looking sad. The lady had found out what Grandma was up to and went to the hospital. She had outsmarted Grandma, and that's saying something.

Third Grade

The summer days quickly went by, John had made himself at home with us in the front bedroom, Terry started changing diapers, and it was time for school to begin again.

I was hoping for another good teacher like Mrs. Robedee. I got Mrs. Brace. She was no Mrs. Robedee, but she wasn't as bad as my first two teachers.

She tried her best to keep me on target, but I couldn't get over the loss of Mrs. Robedee. It didn't take me long to go back to my old habits, and things fell downhill quickly. I was doing the things in school—drawing sailing ships, looking out the window and daydreaming—that allowed me to escape from the classrooms of my first two teachers.

Mrs. Brace gave up bothering me. As long as I behaved, she left me alone. I liked her, so I tried to be good.

She did talk to Mom about getting my eyes tested. Mom said she would.

She didn't right away because there wasn't enough money to go to an eye doctor or pay for glasses if I needed them.

Mom was too busy with little ones to keep after me about school. She still worked at her usual fast pace, but there was something different about her. I could feel it, but I couldn't understand it.

Hurricane Hazel

The news spread quickly around Stump City that a big hurricane was headed our way. The weathermen didn't know where it would hit, but knew it would be here in a few days. Dad tried to act unconcerned about it. I could tell by the way he looked and acted that he was worried.

Mom had no idea what a hurricane was or could do. Terry, Pat, and I listened in as Dad told her.

Mom looked very worried when he said it was stronger than a North Atlantic storm that would hit England once in a while.

Dad said he'd "batten down the hatches" around the house just in case the storm came through our neck of the woods. He put away everything that was loose in the yard, including our toys in the sandbox and our tricycles. I knew it took a strong gust of wind to blow over my tricycle. If a hurricane could blow it away, it told me something about the force of the wind in one.

A few days later on a hot, muggy afternoon and only hours before it hit, we learned on the radio that the giant storm was headed right for Central New York. We already knew something bad was coming because we were getting strong gusts of wind out of the south.

Mom told us to stay in the yard and away from the huge poplar tree in front of the house. She was afraid that a big branch might snap and kill one of us.

We played in the backyard and Prince wouldn't let us out of his sight. The rooster wasn't on border patrol. He was hunkered down in his dog house.

When the winds got steadily stronger, we stood at the top of the hill and the proper distance from the rooster's territory and leaned against it. We could lean way over and got laughing when one of us fell when we leaned too far and the wind let up quickly.

We all ran down the hill to see Dad as he pulled into the driveway and put the car into the garage. He and the rest of the office workers had been let out of work early. After he got out of the car, he took a head count, and we all went into the house together.

It was still daytime, but it was quickly getting dark. Mom turned on the kitchen light and it flickered. Dad went into the basement to get the old hurricane lamp that we used when the lights went off. After he got it, he took it out to the tool shed and filled it up with kerosene.

While we ate supper, we listened to the wind and made small talk. Mealtimes were usually pretty noisy, but not this one. We listened to the windows rattling and the house moaning when a strong gust hit.

The light in the kitchen went out just as we finished eating. Dad fired up the lamp and we did the dishes by its light.

I was old enough to dry and put away dishes by this time and doing it by lamplight was different, so it made it fun.

After the kitchen was cleaned up, we all went into the living room and sat down. Even Chris was quiet and sat on my lap without making a fuss. Prince stayed close to Terry.

Mom had closed all the curtains in the house just in case a window broke. It was eerie in the room with the lamplight flickering.

When the power briefly came back on, Dad tried to tune in a radio station, but between the static on the air waves and the noise of the wind, no one could understand what the voice on the radio was saying.

Dad turned it off, and we all sat there in silence looking at the strange shadows the lamplight made on the ceiling and walls.

I tried not to look scared. Inside I was shaking like the limbs on the poplar tree out front.

It didn't take long for the full force of the storm to hit. The rain was coming down like I'd never seen it before, and the wind sounded worse than a fast freight train going down the main line in Jordan.

Now we were all very scared and Dad knew it. He would almost have to yell for us to hear him as he tried his best to calm us.

Just as if a faucet had been turned off, it became suddenly calm and the rain stopped. I looked at Dad with a puzzled expression. He told us that we were in the eye of the storm and that it was half over. Half over! It seemed like we'd been in the storm for at least a day.

He got up and told us to follow him. We all went out the back door and up to the top of the hill. The small maple tree next to the rooster's home had broken off half-way up. The rooster had his head stuck out of the doghouse. He looked scared. That amazed me. I think I could have gone right into his territory without him even thinking about leaving his place of safety.

We stood there looking up at the beautiful blue sky. When we looked down a bit, we could see the black clouds to the north and west but only blue to the east and south.

Mom let us play, but we had to stay close to her. Dad and Prince just kept staring off to the south.

I wondered if the look-outs on a ship during World War II had the same focused stare that Dad and Prince now had.

After a few minutes he turned towards us and said in a calm voice, "Kids, it's time to get back inside."

We knew that he meant it, so we didn't dilly-dally at all.

We were inside no more than ten minutes when the storm hit us again. This time it seemed even worse than it did before.

It was getting close to bedtime, so Mom, with Dad carrying the lamp and a candle, took us up. We got in bed, and said our prayers and good nights. Mom didn't even bother to tell us to settle down quickly like she always did before. Mom and Dad went back downstairs with Mom carrying Chris. Chris was quiet as a mouse and not complaining or squirming around at all.

We four just lay there not saying a word because we'd have to yell to be heard. I think all of us were watching the candle flicker.

I could feel the house moving a bit, and once in a while a nail would pop with a loud noise. The huge poplar out front made lots of noise with the wind hitting it.

I got up out of bed once to look out. In the strange colored darkness I looked through the rain-streaked windowpane and could see huge limbs moving back and forth. I got back in bed and prayed that the poplar tree wouldn't fall on the house or the house itself wouldn't blow away.

Gradually the wind died down. I don't know when the storm passed because I fell asleep when I thought we might all live through it.

We all got up early, got dressed, and went outside to see what had happened. There was a piece of someone's roof on our lawn, and many branches were scattered on our neighbors' lawns. A power line was down up the street. Dad told us not to go near it.

We followed Dad around the house as he looked up at the roof from all sides. He told us that it was still all there.

I ran out back to see what damage had been done. The doghouse was gone!

I yelled to Dad, and he came at a trot to see what had happened. We looked around, and Dad spotted the doghouse way over by Mr. Moore's hedgerow. We walked over to it. The house was upside down. The rooster was standing inside on his new floor. His feathers were every which way and his eyes had fear in them. He was in shock because he didn't try to peck at Dad when he reached in and lifted him out.

By then, Terry was there. He handed the rooster to her and went to get the wheelbarrow. I helped Dad load the doghouse onto the barrow and balanced it while Dad wheeled it back to its usual spot. Terry then put the thing back inside and went looking for its feed and water bowls.

Lots of electric lines were down and the telephones weren't working in the area. It took many days for everything to get back to normal.

We enjoyed the lamp and candles for a few days but got anxious for the power to come back on. We all missed listening to the radio.

It took the rooster a good day to get back to being his old

self. He forgot about the storm and returned to keeping an eye on his territory.

Not Silent, But Deadly Anyway

On the way home from school in late fall, a strange thing happened. It was very windy and the temperature was dropping. Just after we let Mel White and his brother and sister off, the bus went around a sharp bend in the road. One of the boys passed gas in a very loud manner, something the rest of us boys admired when it was done. Just as he passed the gas, the old barn next to the road went crashing down. We kept looking at the barn and then the boy who had done it. It was an amazing feat.

I was a witness to something most young boys dream about—the power to do something nobody else can do and make it look easy at the same time.

The only drawback for the boy who did it was we all tried to keep a safe distance away from him. He had a deadly weapon that could be fired without warning. If he could destroy a barn, what could he do to us?

Guess Who's Coming to Dinner?

The neighborhood was finally getting back to normal, most of the tree limbs had been picked up and burned, and I was starting to get settled into my school routine.

Mom called for me. The garbage can was full and she wanted me to burn the bits in the burn barrel. I gathered all the burn stuff and got the box matches from the top of the stove.

When I got outside, I noticed that a breeze was kicking up, so I kept the paper bags full of stuff close together. Just as I got to the burn barrel, a strong gust of wind caught me by surprise.

A wad of paper went flying. I tossed the bags into the barrel and ran after the paper.

I wasn't paying attention and had invaded the rooster's territory. Before I realized my mistake, he was after me in a full run with his head down parallel to the ground and his sharp beak pointed straight at me like the sights on a gun. That big bird could fly on his feet.

I turned and ran for the house with the rooster right on my heels. He was too close to me by the time I got to the back door, so I took a quick right and went around the house and down the hill between McEneny's house and ours.

I picked up a good head of steam on the hill. I was really flying, and the sound coming from my mouth resembled an out-of-tune police siren. I glanced to my left and saw Mom looking out of the kitchen window with her mouth open and her eyes wide as I streaked by.

Somehow I made it to the porch and into the kitchen before the rooster got up the porch steps. The door slammed behind me as I ran into Mom's arms. I was shaking and crying while I held Mom around her waist. The rooster was pecking at the door!

We were facing the window, and the rooster was now sitting on the porch railing looking at us with his evil eyes. Mom looked back at him with killing eyes.

I didn't dare go back to the burn barrel and start a fire. Once in a while I'd climb the stairs to look out the hall window. The rooster was back by his doghouse and on border patrol.

When Dad got home from work, Mom told him what had happened.

Dad just said, "Okay, I'll take care of it."

Dad went upstairs and got changed into old work clothes,

came down, and went out the back door with determination in his walk.

A few minutes later I could hear him calling me from out back. I looked out the screen door and slowly opened it. I was afraid that the rooster would get me.

Dad was standing by the tool shed. He didn't say anything. He just waved for me to come out.

When I got next to him he said, "Michael, he won't be putting fear into you or anyone else anymore."

I followed his finger as he was saying this. The rooster was tied to the clothesline with string around his feet and hanging upside down. Dad had wrung his neck.

Old Prince was sitting right underneath him. I could swear he was smiling.

I didn't feel at all bad about seeing the rooster in this condition. I felt relieved.

It's a good thing that Terry was at the Calnon house playing with John. She didn't love the rooster, but it wasn't just another animal to her either.

While I was up tending the fire in the trash barrel, Mom came out with hot water, got the rooster off the line, and came up by me. She poured the hot water over the rooster and then began to pluck him. Finishing that job, she got a Camillus Cutlery pocketknife out of her apron, opened it, and cleaned him. She threw his guts into the fire.

I didn't feel sorry about what was happening to the rooster, but I wasn't happy about it either. Part of the rooster was burning in its own place of damnation. The eatable part would soon be cooking on top of the stove.

When Terry got back from visiting John a few hours later, she asked Mom what was for supper.

Mom said, "We're having boiled chicken in onions and potatoes."

Terry said, "Chicken! We haven't had chicken in a long time."

Mom, Dad, and I didn't tell Terry or the young ones at the table where the chicken had come from. The only comment, and it was repeated often, was, "This chicken sure is tough."

Dad finally said, "'T' is tougher where there isn't any."

As I sat there chewing and chewing just to get a mouthful down, I thought of how the rooster was still giving me problems.

While we were doing the dishes, Mom told Terry about the rooster.

Terry went upstairs in a hurry and cried for a while.

Terry was pretty strong for a girl. She kept the meat in her belly and didn't have to run to the bathroom.

More on the Waltons

Around Thanksgiving time, Davy Walton told me that his father and older brother, Johnny, were going to drive to Arizona to check out jobs. He said that if they found good ones, they might be moving to Arizona.

This took me back a bit, but I hoped that they wouldn't find good jobs and the Walton clan would stay in Stump City.

More on The Drink

"The Drink" continued to play a major part in our lives, but we were getting used to it. I didn't talk to anyone about how much it bothered me. I kept it all bottled up inside of me. For the most part, Mom had given up arguing with Dad. She still wouldn't talk to him for several days after he had come home drunk. I would do the same hoping that he would feel hurt enough to quit. It didn't work.

I still worried myself to death about Dad getting himself home without being killed in a car wreck, and I would not go to sleep until I heard him crawl into bed. Sometimes he was out with the boys until after midnight. I'd be very tired the next day but grateful that he had made it home safely.

Mrs. Mooney

One of the oldest people in the whole world—Mrs. Mooney—lived in Stump City. She lived on Phillips Road behind the Walton house.

Mom had to go there to deliver something, and she had us all in tow. On the way, Mom cautioned us to be mindful of our manners and to keep the noise level down to a dull roar—which meant being quiet for us.

Mrs. Mooney's oldest daughter, who had never married, answered Mom's knock at the door. She was somewhere in her 80's. Her younger brother, Jim, who was also single, was inside. The two of them took us to see their mother.

Mrs. Mooney was propped up in her bed with large feather pillows and covered with a comforter.

I've never seen anything like it in my whole life! She had beautiful, shiny, white hair that was well-combed and covered most of the pillow. Her face was mildly plump and had very few wrinkles. She smiled when she realized that people had come to call on her. I swear that she'd have had a twinkle in her eyes if she wasn't blind.

Mom began to talk to her in a normal voice. There was a tone of respect that I'd only hear her use when she spoke to Reverend McMahon, another priest, or a nun. I thought for sure she'd have to yell because that is what she'd have to do when she talked to most older people.

We children just stood there looking at the beautiful old woman. Mom talked to her for quite a while, but none of us moved or even took a jab at someone. The warmth and love in the room almost overwhelmed us.

After Mom had said good-bye and had us do the same, we started walking home. I broke the silence by asking Mom how old Mrs. Mooney was. Mom told us that she was 105. She added that Mrs. Mooney was in her teens when President Lincoln's funeral train came through Syracuse in 1865 and could still remember with sadness the day the train went by with thousands of people silently standing by the railroad tracks.

Bad News in the Third Grade

I guess I didn't understand school reasoning very well after all. On the last day of school we all got our report cards to take home. Since I liked Mrs. Brace and we got along well enough, I wasn't too worried about passing. After all, I had passed before without doing much.

I was in for a big surprise as I stood before Mom with my report card. She looked at the grades, turned it over to see what Mrs. Brace had written, and looked at me.

"Michael, I'm very disappointed in you. You have failed the grade and will have to repeat it again next year."

She wasn't angry, but I could see that she was disappointed in me. That hurt like a knife slicing through my heart. It hurt even more than the thought of repeating. I was completely crushed.

I thought about Mom's look, my friends who would be

moving on, and how I had felt about kids who had failed. I believed they were really dumb.

I was joining the crowd.

Michael Gets Glasses

Dad said that he had come up with the money to have my eye examination. He took me to a house in Weedsport to be checked over by Dr. Stapleton. He had his office in his huge house.

I stood next to Dad after the exam. Dr. Stapleton said that I had a lazy eye and needed glasses. He told Dad to bring me back next week for the glasses and an eye patch.

When I put them on for the first time and the doctor made me read something, I could do it without my eyes hurting. I didn't like to read in school because I'd get eye aches.

The pain would often make me ask Mom to stay home. Sometimes she'd let me.

One time when I had to go to school with the pain, I asked the teacher if I could go to the nurse, Mrs. Bowen. She wrote me a pass.

I quickly learned that teachers let students go to the nurse's office when they asked. Many times I was feeling just fine. It was a good way to get out of class and go lie down for a nap. If I acted sick enough, Mrs. Bowen would take me home in the yellow school station wagon. I would have to stay in the bedroom until school was out, but that was okay with me.

Mom knew what was going on, but didn't say much about it. She knew I didn't like school.

I'd have to wear the glasses all day. It didn't take me long to get used to them. Every day Mom would place the patch on the lens of my good eye and have me keep it on for fifteen minutes. She said that it would make my lazy eye work and the muscles in it would get stronger. It seemed to help.

Harry Joyce Returns

The brightest part of the summer was Harry Joyce. He came to visit for two or three days. He had presents for each of us. I don't remember what he gave me. The best present was Mr. Joyce himself.

The whole house seemed to cheer up. We were sad to see him leave, but we knew we would be.

It was hard to say good-bye to someone I loved and admired so much.

The Five-Day Vacation Theory, Part IV

Mom started wearing baggy shirts again. She was really getting even with Dad for keeping her up late.

I kept an eye on Mom to see if she was getting the same look she had the last time she wore the baggy shirts. I didn't want her to have to go back into the hospital except to have babies. She didn't have the spring in her step that she used to have, but she seemed okay. I was relieved.

Where was Chris going to sleep after he got kicked out? I decided not to think about it.

Mom Learns to Drive

With one car and no driver's license, Mom felt trapped in the house and she told Dad so. Dad decided that it was time for Mom to learn how to drive.

At first, Dad would take Mom out to the car and explain the use of the clutch, the different places for each gear, and let her practice without starting up the engine. When he felt she was ready to get on the road, he would have her drive up and down our dead-end street in first or second gear. We'd stand on the porch and watch all of this. It was like watching a daredevil act in a circus.

Mom would give it too much gas and the car would buck forward causing both of their heads to snap back and forth. Once Mom got the car going, she liked to drive on the wrong side of the road because that's the way people did it in England.

Dad would get all excited and start saying bad words when Mom almost killed them both, which seemed often. Mom would then storm out of the car, slam the door, and walk back to the house.

After a week or so of watching the show, Dad decided that Mom could drive on other roads. We always wanted to go for a ride in the car, but this wasn't going to be just any ride. We all tried to be the last one in the car to delay the start.

Once we were all in the back seat, Mom started the engine. I started to pray to St. Christopher, the guardian saint of drivers. Just getting started at the top of our hill at the stop sign took a couple of minutes because Mom wouldn't give the car enough gas to get moving on the slight hill, or she'd panic a bit if the car started rolling back and pop the clutch.

We all learned to brace ourselves so we wouldn't get our necks hurt.

Dad told Mom to turn left once she got the car moving. The road went down a hill and took a mean left curve to go over the narrow bridge above Skaneateles Creek.

I thought for sure Mom wouldn't make it, and she wouldn't have had Dad not grabbed the wheel just a second before we went over the bank and into the creek.

The rest of the lesson didn't go much better. Mom would stall out at every stop sign. Dad would have to grab the wheel and jerk the car back onto the road and off someone's lawn several times.

Dad's tongue had a hard time keeping the language clean, but he managed somehow to control it.

We all jumped out of the car when we got back home. I was so relieved that I almost got down on my hands and knees to thank St. Christopher for answering my prayers, which were flowing freely for the whole ride.

Even Chris was scared. I could tell because he had a death grip around Terry's neck.

For at least two months we put our lives in Mom's hands every Sunday afternoon. These rides were sure not like the ones Dad took us on before.

Mom felt that she was ready for her road test. Dad didn't, and my neck didn't either. Mom won out and got an appointment for a test in Auburn.

Dad took her over there on the test day while we stayed next door with the McEnenys.

They came back a few hours later with Dad behind the wheel. Mom wasn't looking very happy, and I didn't dare ask. She never did tell us what happened.

Later in the week, she got a letter saying she had failed the test. Dad wasn't at all surprised, but he kept his mouth shut.

Dad had to give her more lessons, and we'd have to come along. Her driving seemed to be getting better, but she still had lots of rough edges to iron out.

After a few more weeks of practice, Mom thought she was ready enough to take the test again.

She failed again!

To make it short, Mom had to take the test four times before she finally passed. She was so happy about passing the test that she used Grandma Quigley's phone to call all her girl-friends to tell them the good news.

Dad told me in a whisper that he thought the driver test man had had enough of Mom and didn't want to get in the car with her again. We both laughed.

I stopped laughing when Mom told me that she wanted me to go to Skaneateles with her to help her do the grocery shopping at the A & P store. It would be her first time driving without Dad next to her.

I didn't dare say no, but I knew I was either going to die or come close to it.

As soon as we got into the car, I started to pray and didn't stop until we were out of the car in Skaneateles. We had made it there without Mom bringing us to the brink of death.

God is good.

The car now loaded with two weeks' worth of groceries, we got back in and headed home. I prayed all the way home.

Mom stayed on her side of the road, didn't have any near misses with other cars or trees, and didn't stall the engine out once.

God is very good.

More on the Railroad

Mom gave me a list of things to get at Cronaeur's Store. I was in no big hurry, so I took the long way there. I heard the diesel train coming up the tracks from Hartlot, but couldn't see it yet.

Just after I had walked past St. Bridget's, it came up behind me. I heard it slow, but didn't look around. It was probably going to pick up a boxcar at the railroad siding by Waterbury Felt Company.

"Mike, do you want to go for a short ride?"

I turned to see the train engineer smiling at me.

I was in a trance. I didn't even bother to answer. I ran over to the engine and climbed aboard.

The engineer pushed the throttle forward and we started to move. I could really feel the power of its engine. The whole cab seemed to rumble. I was in heaven. There were many gauges that meant nothing to me except for the rpm and fuel gauges.

He didn't say a word to me nor did I to him. We just smiled at each other. It was a short ride, but it was a ride in the cab of a train. He stopped at Cronaeur's Store. I remembered to thank him as I climbed down the ladder.

It wasn't a ride in the cab of one of the old steamers, but it was the next best thing.

The Five-Day Vacation Theory, Part V

I have to admit that I had been a fool about babies coming out of a mom's belly button. How could I believe in such nonsense? Older kids don't know everything, and I wouldn't be so easily taken in by one of them again.

A boy in my class set me straight. He told me in a very serious, quiet voice that babies came from a mom's bottom. It made perfect sense because I had stood up from the toilet and seen some mighty large things in the bowl.

It was sickening to think that babies were born that way. Who would want to be a baby doctor? Why, he was nothing more than a septic tank cleaning man with a higher education.

I felt sorry for the poor nurses who were made to work on

the Baby Floor of a hospital. How could most of them be smiling every time we went to visit Mom in the hospital?

Rocky

Terry loved horses and spent any free time she had with Charlotte Walters who lived up a bit on Stump Road. Charlotte loved horses too and had one. She and Terry would spend hours riding and tending to the horse.

Dad surprised us all when he came home with a horse for Terry. He got the horse at the Sennett Sales Auction.

The horse's name was Rocky. He was a small pinto with a good disposition, as Dad liked to say.

Dad fixed up a stall in one area of the tool shed, ran electric fence around the small field behind the house, and hooked up a powerful weed chopper to put electricity through the wire. It was called a weed chopper because when weeds grew tall enough to touch the wire, they got burned off.

It kept Rocky in the field, and he learned how to put his head and neck under it so he could reach the fresh grass on the lawn. Once in a while he'd get greedy and try to stretch too far under the fence by getting on his knees. If his mane touched the wire, Rocky would get big eyes and bolt away from the fence. His hind legs would give a swift kick in the direction of the fence, and he'd violently shake his head like a boxer who took a hard hit to his nose.

Dad told Terry she was in charge of feeding, watering, brushing, and cleaning out Rocky's stall.

She loved to do all but one of these tasks. Over a period of time she began to be less and less fond of cleaning the stall.

Somehow I got the job.

I'd load the wheelbarrow up, push it to the garden area, and spread the manure around. It's amazing how much a horse can have come out of its business end.

One day I was currycombing the horse with the metal brush. I shouldn't have been doing it because I could see a steady downward workload for Terry and a rising one for me, but I liked to do it once in a while. Rocky seemed to enjoy it.

As I brushed Rocky's haunches, something must have upset him and he moved his butt quickly. The currycomb came out of my hand. Just as I bent down to pick it up, Rocky kicked me hard with a back leg and I went flying.

I pulled myself up off the ground crying and rubbing my cheek. I went limping and crying to the house to tell Mom what had happened.

My finger was cut where I had hit it on the metal brush, so Mom rinsed it out and put peroxide on it. She then had me pull down my pants to see what damage the horse had done. She said there was a perfect horseshoe mark. To prove it to me, she got a hand mirror.

It looked just like the kind I'd seen on cartoons at the movies when some character got kicked by a horse or a mule.

I quickly got over the pain in my rear, but my nail started looking funny and started to fall out. I wondered what Rocky was carrying to cause that to happen.

Mom got upset that I hadn't told her anything about it. She told me to get into the car because she wanted Dr. Horne to look at it.

Dr. Horne told me that I was very lucky that I didn't get lockjaw. He finished off my visit by giving me a tetanus shot.

Third Grade-Again

Summer was about over. I had three big reasons to fear going back: I was afraid of what the kids would say on the bus about me going through third grade again, being teased and called "four eyes," and being with kids I didn't know. I was really feeling the pressure and didn't have much fun during the last week of summer vacation.

The only fear that came true was being called "four eyes." When the kids got used to me in glasses, the ribbing stopped. I think the glasses drew their attention away from the fact that I had flunked third grade.

It took a while to make new friends and get over not seeing old school friends—maybe a week or so.

For some reason, I can't remember my teacher's name. Anyway, I buckled down and was determined to do a much better job. I didn't want Mom to worry about me, and I sure didn't want to fail again.

To my great surprise, it didn't hurt to read, and we did a lot of that. The headaches were almost all gone.

Looking out the window became less of a temptation, but I still liked to draw. Now I liked to draw old steam locomotives.

I did most of my work and paid attention to the teacher most of the time.

It was going to be a good year; I could feel it in my bones.

Turkey Necks and Chicken Wings

In late fall, Dad got a job at Jimmy O'Hara's meat market in Weedsport. He only worked on Saturdays. He didn't come home late very often now because he had to get up early every Saturday morning and didn't get home until around seven.

The job brought in extra money for the growing family and took the tension level down in the house several notches.

When Dad got home from the meat market, he'd always have a big steak with him. While he was getting his smelly clothes off, washing up, and putting clean clothes on, Mom would fry up the steak in a pan with potatoes and onions.

The smell made my mouth water. Good steak was non-existent in our house until Dad started working at the meat market.

We'd sit at the table talking to Dad as he slowly ate. He'd give us each a small piece. He knew I liked the fat the best, so I would get all of it. He said the fat upset his stomach.

Most of the time, Dad was too tired to go out. That made us all happy.

I started sleeping better and my stomachaches stopped after he started working for Mr. O'Hara.

Working at the meat market had another benefit that was both good and bad. Once every month or so, Mr. O'Hara would give Dad a huge bag of turkey necks.

At first we all loved them. The newness wore off in short order, but we were forced to eat them. Mom would say, "'T'is that or nothing." We knew she meant it.

We went for at least a month without having to eat any more turkey necks. We all thought that we were home clear. We were wrong. The big push for turkey was over. Mr. O'Hara was now sending huge packages of chicken wings home with Dad. It took us a little longer to get tired of them than it did the turkey necks.

We had learned by now that it didn't do any good to complain about what was set before us. We bit our tongues and ate.

Between all the necks and wings we had to eat, it's a wonder that we didn't all grow up looking like some strange versions of giraffes with wings.

Cold Metal and a Wet Hand

It was very cold one Sunday morning, and Mom made sure we were all bundled up. We hurried to church and sat down in our usual pew on the left side. The Walton family was in front of us. They were taking up a whole pew. I think they already had about eight or nine kids.

Would Mom catch up?

Very few people took off their coats in church and the pews were always filled. One of the ushers, Mr. Gray, had his hands full just trying to get latecomers all seated. Even the choir loft would have many people in it. If people came in late, they had to stand in the back. Many times men would get up and let women take their seats. They'd walk to the back and stand for the service.

Missing church on Sunday was a mortal sin. I had learned in Sunday school that "mortal" meant deadly. I figured that the church was always crowded because people didn't want to commit a very bad sin and have to tell the priest about it when they went to confession. I know I wouldn't.

The heat in the church would be mortal too. Many times I sat there wondering if the heat would kill me before the service ended.

That Sunday was almost mortal to me. I couldn't wait to get outside into the cold air. While Mom and Dad talked to people, I hurried outside. I forgot to put my gloves on. Halfway down the many steps, my right hand suddenly stuck to the metal railing. Before I could stop myself from hitting the next step, my hand ripped away from it. A sudden pain shot through my whole body. I looked at my hand and a bunch of skin was missing. I looked at the railing and found my missing skin. I wanted to shout out in pain and cry, but I didn't.

I put my gloves on, turned my head away from people so they couldn't see my face, and let a tear or two trickle down my cheeks.

When the rest of the family finally caught up with me, I walked home in silence. I didn't dare say anything to Mom about my hand because I was supposed to have my gloves on before I got outside. I suffered for several days.

I learned something about science. And I learned that Mom was right about wearing gloves in cold weather.

Christmas 1954 and Sledding

For Christmas Santa left me a beautiful new American Flyer sled. It was much longer than the little one I got from Rose McEneny and had rounded-up runners in the back. Now I couldn't stab myself in the leg with the end of a runner when I took a nasty roll. I could also get my whole body, except for my feet, onto the sled. It was better to have toes hanging over the back edge because they would help me make very quick turns. My feet were used as rudders.

Terry got my old sled. She and I would stay outside for a very long time speeding down the hill and running back up to do it all over again.

Pat and John were too small to last long outside. I'd take

them down one at a time either sitting between my legs or holding onto my back for dear life.

The hard part was pulling them back up. I'd make them walk on the flat part and then load them onto the sled when they couldn't get any further up the hill. They'd start to put on lots of weight after a few trips up the hill. When I got tired of pulling them back up, I'd ask them if they'd had enough or if they were cold. The planted seed would grow, and shortly after, they would usually say they were getting cold and wanted to go back inside.

Terry and I would bring them to the back door and yell for Mom. She'd come out with the house broom and brush the snow off and take them inside for a cup of very weak tea to get them warmed up to their normal operating temperatures.

Terry and I would continue going up and down until I was too tired to do it any more. She would want to stay out longer, but I just couldn't drag myself up the hill again. The towing jobs I had done for Pat and John had taken the wind out of my sails. Terry thought she was tougher.

I didn't bother arguing with her. It wasn't worth the effort. Besides, she could wear me down by out-talking me and win the argument anyway.

Mom would come to the door with the broom and do her job on us. Since we were older, she wasn't as gentle with us. Once in a while I'd get a scratch on my face when she was in too much of a hurry to finish the brushing.

We'd take off our clothes in the back room. Often my dungarees were so stiff that I could stand them up. My legs would be beet red. The hot, weak tea would thaw us out some. Standing close to the coal stove would finish the job in short order.

The Arrival of the Telephone

Every time Dad or Mom used a phone, they either had to go to the McEneny or Quigley house. When I asked Mom or Dad about why we didn't have a phone, they said that we couldn't afford one.

When I was getting off the bus one day, I looked down the street and saw a telephone repair truck in front of our house. We all ran down to the house to see if the telephone man was there to ask if we wanted a phone or was putting one in.

Before we got to the house, I knew we were getting a phone. On the ground there was a shiny, black line leading from the electric pole to our house.

We quietly watched the repairman as he put a wire from the wall to the back of the phone. When he was done doing that, we followed him outside, and watched him put on spikes, climb the pole like a monkey, and connect some wires. We followed him back into the house like little puppies following someone carrying a bowl of milk.

We all went silent, even Mom, as he lifted the phone.

The person on the other end must have asked him how he sounded because he said, "Loud and clear."

He hung up the phone and told Mom to be very careful with it because phones could and did break.

Before he was back to his truck, Mom picked up the phone. All of us were standing real close. She placed her finger to her lips for silence and swished us back a bit. She put the phone up to her ear, waited a moment, and said, "Overbrook 377J2, please."

"Hello, Helen, this is Ethel."

Mom had called Mrs. McEneny! I couldn't understand why she had called someone so close. All she had to do was stick her head out the window and give her a yell. I would have called someone like Harry Joyce who lived far away.

Mom didn't know much about giving new gadgets a really good test.

I can't remember ever using the phone until I was much older and had school friends who lived too far away. I would always just walk to a friend's house, knock on the door, and say, "Is So and So in, Mrs. So and So?"

The biggest problem Mom had was getting an open line. We were on a party line with at least six other families in the neighborhood. Mom would lift up the phone very carefully, put it to her ear to see if the line was busy, and put it down quietly when someone was using it.

It was often busy because we had one neighbor who felt naked unless the phone was by her ear. If this lady wanted to use the phone, she would just pick it up and say, "This is an emergency, please get off the phone."

Mom knew who it was and would get very angry. Mom would get off the phone because the law said that if a person had an emergency call to make, the person using the line must hang up.

To this day, I still pick up the phone and listen to see if someone is on the line before I dial a number. It's hard to break old habits.

I was almost as excited about a phone in our house as I was when Mr. Manley seemed to take forever putting in the indoor plumbing.

When I really think about it, the indoor plumbing beat a telephone by a long shot. It was much easier for me to deliver a message to a neighbor than it was to sit on a cold seat in the wintertime with fumes worse than any baby diaper I'd ever smelled attacking my nose.

Television Arrives in Stump City—Part I

Davy Walton told me on the bus that his dad might be getting a television set. I couldn't believe it! Mr. Walton worked very hard to support his family, and his family was bigger than ours. How could this be? Did a rich old uncle leave him money? To top it off, Mr. Walton's one-legged dad was living with them.

It was just beyond belief, and I told Davy so.

The subject was dropped, and I didn't think about it much.

Less than a week had passed and we were on the bus. Davy leaned over and told me that there was a television in his house.

I knew he was telling the truth because if he was joshing me, he'd always wipe the corner of his mouth, and his left eye would twitch if he was trying to tell me a whopper.

He told me about the television, and I listened with both ears fully open.

He said that it was an amazing thing to see people walking and talking in a box. Davy also said that he and the rest of his family, including his grandfather, sat in front of it last night and watched whatever was on without saying a word.

That really impressed me because the Walton house was never quiet until some time after ten at night. I had to see this thing!

Davy invited me to come up and take a look at it myself after school.

The school day dragged by. It wasn't a good day for me

because I just couldn't think straight enough to get much done. I kept imagining what it must be like to watch a television.

When we finally got on the bus that afternoon, I told Davy that I'd be over after I asked Mom if I could. I prayed that Mom didn't have anything for me to do.

For a change, she didn't. My prayer was answered.

I ran up the road as fast as I could, knocked on the door, and asked his older sister, Penny, if Davy was home. She said that he was in the barn doing his chores.

When I got to the barn, Davy was busy cleaning the cow's pen. The Waltons had so many kids that it was cheaper to keep a cow than it was to pay Mr. Hudson to deliver milk to the house.

It didn't take him long to finish up because his only other chore was feeding the billy goat and that was easy.

We both hustled back to the house, went inside, and Davy turned on the television. It didn't come on!

Davy and I hustled into the kitchen to ask his mom what was wrong with it. His mom said that a tube had blown and it would have to be fixed.

What a disappointment!

I asked Davy how long it took to get a new tube. He didn't know.

We both found out that it took over a week before a repairman could come and replace it.

After it was fixed, Davy invited me into the house to see the television. I held my breath when Davy turned it on. It worked! I couldn't believe my eyes. People were moving around just like Davy had said they would. The picture wasn't clear, but it didn't matter.

I sat there looking at the box like a kid looking at a five pound piece of chocolate. I didn't know or care what the people were doing. Just seeing them in a box looking very small but alive was more than enough for me.

This was beyond a telephone and indoor plumbing. I would very easily give up both and go back to the old ways without batting an eye if we had a television in our house.

I knew it would be a long wait before the day came when I could see people in a box in our own living room.

I didn't pester Mom and Dad about getting one. I knew it would get them angry because I was asking for something so expensive.

Thanksgiving 1955

Thanksgiving Day that year was held at Aunt Pat's and Uncle Danny's house. There were just too many of us now for the grandparents' house to hold and have any kind of elbow room.

Grandma Quigley was all bundled up, wheeled over to the house, and hoisted up the porch steps with great care by Uncle Jimmy and Dad.

This was like a voyage for her. I'd never seen her leave the property much. Once in a while Aunt Ann would wheel her down the road a bit and back up to the house. If a neighbor was out at the time, Grandma would nod and listen to what the neighbor had to say. She knew it was useless for her to talk because only Aunt Mary had the gift of truly understanding her.

Grandpa Quigley wasn't moving around much. Dad had to help him across the street and up the front porch steps. I watched Dad help him. He was very gentle with him. It made me begin to worry about Grandpa.

Anyway, it wasn't uncommon for Uncle Jim and Uncle Danny to start up singing when the big meal was finished, and they'd had a drop or two. They sang very well together. Everyone would start clapping and yelling after they had finished a song.

One of the older folks—I think Aunt Pat—came up with the idea of having us little ones sing a song for them. I stood in the back mumbling the words to the song while my sisters took center stage. They sang loud enough to drown out what I was mumbling from the back. I couldn't sing at all.

The feeling I had in Aunt Pat's and Uncle Danny's house was different than the one I had in my grandparents' house. It was a feeling of life. Part of it came from how Aunt Pat and Uncle Danny acted around one another. The rest came from not having to see all the "old people things" scattered around the Grandparents' house.

Things were headed uphill in the Calnon home, while things were headed downhill across the street.

I wonder if anyone else felt it too.

Christmas 1955

My sisters, brothers, and I wrote notes to Santa again and put them into the stove. I was getting suspicious about this means of talking to Santa because I was hearing more stories on the bus. Many of the older kids thought it was funny that I believed in Santa. They had stopped believing long before they reached my age and were still getting presents. The doubts placed in my head were still being shut down, but not completely, because of what happened when I got the electric train set and the sled for the last two Christmases.

All my doubts vanished when I got a Roy Rogers cap gun and holster. It even came with bullets in the gun belt that looked real.

I had only told Mom, Dad, and Santa when I burned my

note and put it into the stove. I had made sure not to tell anyone else, not even Terry, so that I could test to see if Santa was real. He passed my test with ease!

Grandpa Quigley Passes

The news that Grandpa had been taken to the hospital came in early January. He had suffered another heart attack.

Would he will himself to get better so he could get home to his easy chair and start chewing tobacco again?

A few days later Dad came home and gently told us that Grandpa Quigley was dead. It was the first time that someone I loved a lot had died, and it shook me to the core.

I would surely miss his grand stories and watching him spit into his spittoon.

After O'Neill's Funeral Home had made him look presentable, he was set up in his Sunday best in the very same spot in the living room where his chair used to be.

Dad and Mom took us all up to see him. I was scared, but this time I wanted to say good-bye and not run right out of the house.

Grandpa looked small in the casket. His face looked different because he didn't have a chewing tobacco stain on the right corner of his mouth and he was clean shaven.

After the funeral mass was held in St. Bridget's Church and he was put to rest in St. Mary's Cemetery, many of Grandpa's relatives, friends, and neighbors came back to Grandma's house for food and drink. It was a quiet affair until several of the men had a wee bit too much of the good Irish whiskey. Then the stories about Grandpa and the "remember when's" started to fly.

Listening to the men folk talk took the edge off Grandpa's death, but only just a little bit.

For a long time after when I was going into Grandma's house, I'd stick my head around the living room door, look at Grandpa's chair, and remember him sitting there and telling me stories. The only thing missing was the brass spittoon.

I missed Grandpa for a long time.

The Waltons Leave Stump City

I was put into instant shock when Mom told me in January 1956 that the Waltons were moving to Arizona. Mr. Walton had lost his job and heard that there were plenty of openings there. Earlier, he and another son, Johnny, had gone to Arizona to look for jobs. Davy was excited about going, but he was also sad about leaving all of his friends behind.

Mr. Walton came back from Arizona in his old car. Johnny was already working and stayed behind. He traded it in for a brand new Chevy station wagon. The old one might have gotten them as far as Buffalo before it died.

On the day they were leaving, we all went up to say goodbye. Mom hugged Mrs. Walton, the girls hugged each other, and I shook Davy's hand.

Somehow all of them got into the wagon, except for Mr. Walton's dad. He had decided to move to a small place in Mexico, New York.

Mrs. Walton sat in the front holding a baby. Another older one sat next to her. Four of the littlest ones were sitting in the very back seat. The rest climbed into the middle seat. The top of the car had a huge mound of stuff on it, and the small trailer behind the wagon was tightly packed.

We all yelled and waved as they slowly went down Stump

Road. I was very sad and cried a little as I watched them disappear down the hill and around the bend just passed the creek bridge.

When they were out of sight, I turned and looked at the empty house. It looked like it was sad too.

It wasn't long after they left when I saw a real estate sign in the front lawn.

I now missed Grandpa and the Waltons.

Johnny O'Hara

We were all walking out of church on a mild February day in 1956, and Johnny O'Hara (he was either a brother or first cousin to Jimmy O'Hara) stopped to say hello to us. We exchanged greetings.

Mr. O'Hara looked at Dad, winked, and said to me, "Michael, me boy, have you seen the butcher lately?"

I was puzzled by the question and said, "No sir, Mr. O'Hara. I haven't seen the butcher."

He let go with a loud belly laugh, said his good-byes, and continued laughing as he walked away.

I looked up at Dad and he just smiled. I could see that I wasn't going to get an answer, so I just let it go.

On the way home, I kept thinking about Mr. O'Hara's strange question.

Every time that I saw Mr. O'Hara after that, he would ask me the same question, and I would give him the same answer. He always laughed. I would smile because of his laughing, which would make him laugh even more. His laughing would make my smile even bigger.

As dense as I was, it took me a very long time to figure out why he would ask me such a strange question. I saw the butcher everyday. The butcher was Dad!

The Five-Day Vacation Theory, Part VI

Toward the middle of March in 1956, Dad took Mom to the hospital. By now Mom was used to the routine and anxious to get out of the house for five days. I could tell because about a week before Dad took her, she packed an old suitcase and had it sitting in the upstairs hallway. The suitcase became a sign of room changes, another mouth to feed, and the house complaining about another body to be sheltered.

Peg

When we asked Dad what the baby's name was, he told us that he knew, but wanted Mom to tell us. He hadn't even told us if it was a boy or a girl.

Going to see a new brother or sister was different this time. Before, I had imagined the baby coming very slowly out of Mom's belly button. The real way they came out sickened me.

If the baby doctors made moms sit on toilets to have their babies, how many had been accidentally flushed away? Even worse, what happened to the babies that slipped through a doctor's hands before indoor plumbing when moms had to go sit in outhouses?

I never heard of any baby being flushed down or drowning in an outhouse in a very awful way.

The baby doctors must be very good at what they have to do—true professionals doing a dirty job.

As usual, we went to see the new baby first. Dad pointed it out to us.

I was so happy! The baby had red hair. It wasn't the same shade as mine, but it didn't matter. Up until now, I was the only redhead in Stump City. (Red Phillips used to have red hair, but it had turned white. He didn't count.)

I was teased about my hair a lot, and I was very tired of being teased. With two redheads in the area, maybe the kids and some grownups would stop teasing me.

I did check the baby out very carefully to see if the nurses had properly cleaned it up. I didn't see any dirty spots on it.

I was relieved to see that Mom was acting okay. After she gave us all hugs, she told us that the baby was a girl and her name was Margaret, but Dad told us to call her Peg because it was Irish for Margaret.

Five to a Room

Chris was thrown out of the bedroom and moved in with us. There were now five of us living in the one, small bedroom.

There wasn't enough room for another bed, so Chris had to bunk with me. At first it was hard to get much sleep because Chris had bony knees that seemed to always hit the center of my back, and he kept moving around like he had a monster chasing him. It took me a good week to ignore him. Maybe I just got too tired to notice.

Mom and Dad could see I wasn't getting much sleep and decided to buy something rare—a new piece of furniture. They got bunk beds.

Chris got the top bunk, I got the bottom bunk, and John got my old steel hospital bed with the chipped white paint.

It's a good thing that the top bunk came with a wooden

safety railing. Chris wouldn't have survived a night without it the way he moved around in bed.

As it was, I had to adjust to the constant movement of the bed because he couldn't stay still even when he was asleep. It was easier to get used to the moving than it was having him in bed with me, and I finally started getting some decent rest.

Michael Passes the Fourth Grade

The school year went by faster than any other had gone by before. I didn't worry at all about passing. It was a good feeling.

Mom and Dad were both pleased with what I had done in school.

When the time came for report cards, I took it home, Mom looked at it, smiled in relief, and told me to go show Grandma Simpson.

Grandma looked at it very carefully and said, "You should have done better in reading. Terry's and Pat's grades are much better."

I didn't feel hurt about what she had said. If she had said, "My, what a wonderful report card," I think I'd have dropped dead from the shock.

It's much better to stay alive than it is to get a pat on the back from Grandma and die from the shock.

Life without praise would be better than death because of it.

More on Chris

Mom told Terry and Patty that they were a good help to her, so she promoted them to lighten her load around the house. They were now in charge of taking care of Chris and Peg. Peg wouldn't be much of a problem, so Pat kept an eye on her and changed her diapers.

Keeping an eye on Chris was serious work, and Terry had to take care of him.

Chris was crawling around the house like he was possessed, and he was into everything. Things that could break were placed very high up.

Chris must have had rubber arms. If Terry took her eyes off him and no one else was looking, there would be the sound of something breaking. How could he reach that high? He must have used his rubber arms only when no one was looking.

The playpen had worked well as a holding area for the rest of us, but Chris found it no challenge to escape.

Chris had a very red bottom for doing and getting into things that he shouldn't. He was a determined boy and wouldn't let a little pain get into the way of what he had his mind set on doing.

Terry was beginning to get Mom's haggard look.

When Chris was taking a nap, Mom would sometimes let Terry and Pat go play with Cousin John and Cousin Mary Kay Calnon. Terry would run up the street with Pat in tow like she was escaping from Hell itself.

She and John were great friends and spent time doing all kinds of different things together.

Aunt Pat had a play area set up in a small room just off the living room. Their house was big enough to have such a place. In our house, any open area where we wouldn't be in the line of traffic would become our play spot. Rarely were we allowed to play in the kitchen, because Mom didn't like us being "under foot" while she worked in there. It's a wonder Mom didn't put a bed in the kitchen. She probably would have done so if there had been the room for one.

With Chris acting like he constantly ate spoonfuls of sugar, I had to quickly set up my train set, play with it, and get it put away before he woke up. It took some of the pretend out of playing because I had to keep an ear open to any sound from upstairs. A rustling in the crib meant that I had to stop and get the tracks taken apart and the train put away.

When Chris learned to walk, things got worse. He was a speed demon. I've never seen a little one move so fast, and by this time I'd seen plenty of babies to know what I was talking about.

Mom put him to bed earlier than she had put John when he was Chris's age. She did this because Chris's sugar supply had run out and he was ready for a long, restless night's sleep.

With Chris in bed, the energy level in the house dropped several notches. I could almost hear the house sighing in relief.

Mowing—Part II

Mom didn't have the strength, time, or the will to mow the lawn now. Dad had to do it when he got home from work.

I knew I was getting stronger, so I asked Dad if I could try mowing. I breezed back and forth across the lawn like nobody's business. It surprised Dad and me that I could push the mower so easily.

Dad had a big smile on his face and said, "Michael, not too many boys can do the mowing like that at your age, especially not on a hill."

I beamed back up at him and stuck my chest out as far as it would go.

Ah, I was so happy.

Dad gave me some pointers on the finer art of mowing and let me go at it. He stuck around long enough to make some minor adjustments in my technique and set me free.

He went to the shed to get his hoe and set off for the garden. I went back to the mowing.

I kept an eye on him while he worked in the garden. Every time he looked my way, I'd speed up a little to show him that I wasn't tired. By the time I was finished, I was in a good lather, tired, and very happy. I was becoming a man by pulling some of the weight around the house.

The really big thing was having Dad say something so grand about me. The good feeling just bubbled and bubbled inside.

The Mumps

A bad sickness Mom called mumps was spreading around Stump City. It didn't take long to visit our house. Dr. Horne was called to the house. After he looked me over, he declared that I did indeed have the mumps. All of us children got sick with it around the same time. We looked like chipmunks because our cheeks were swollen. It really hurt to swallow.

I don't remember much about having the mumps because it really knocked me and the rest of house on our backs. I do remember being in bed listening to kids crying, moaning and groaning, and calling for Mom. It was dark in the room too because Mom said any bright light could cause us to go blind. I made sure to keep my eyes shut most of the time. I didn't want to end up like Mrs. Olmstead or Mrs. Mooney. Mom was exhausted from all the caring she had to do.

She and Dad looked worried until every last one of us recovered.

The whole summer seemed to center around sickness and chasing Chris around the house.

Michael Starts the Fifth Grade

Mrs. McCarthy was my fifth grade teacher. I don't remember much about her or the school year. That's good, because it means that school went like clock work.

The only thing that really stands out in my mind about the school year was what happened on the bus one day. I was sitting towards the front of the bus and we had just arrived at school. A girl across the aisle lost her breakfast. (I had enough trouble myself because I was always getting bus sick. I had always managed to keep breakfast down, but I really had to concentrate on it.) The smell and the sight was more than my weak stomach could take. I heaved all over the poor girl sitting right in front of me. The chain reaction had started. Two more kids saw what had happened and lost their morning meals too.

If the girl who had thrown up first and I were sitting at the back of the bus, the whole bus would have been going at it.

Mr. Hill, our bus driver, was a smart man. He scrambled out of his seat, quickly went out the door, and ran to the back of the bus. At first I thought he was just escaping the scene. He opened the emergency exit door at the rear of the bus and unloaded the kids seated in the back before they started to join the breakfast hurling contest.

He saved the kids in the back from the contest and saved himself a very messy cleanup.

He certainly was one quick-thinking man.

It was weird, because Mrs. McCarthy had said something about the domino effect a few weeks earlier when a boy in class started laughing and, one after the other, we all did too.

I liked the laughing effect much better than the throwing up one.

The nurse had a full load of students to take home right after she figured out the student attendance for that day.

I bet she was looking in the rear view mirror for any signs that the unpleasant activity on the bus was starting up again.

The Five-Day Vacation Theory, Part VII

Late in the fall, Mom was wearing baggy shirts again. I had caught onto the two-year pattern for baggy shirts by now because I knew in what year each of us was born. I was looking for the baggy shirt weeks before Mom started wearing it.

I couldn't figure out why Mom wanted to go through having another baby after what I had learned a few years ago and seeing how each new brother or sister was wearing her down a bit more.

Was it because she was desperate for five-day vacations or did she want to be known around Stump City as being smarter than Mrs. Walton or because she wanted to get even with Dad for keeping her up late at nights?

More on Peg

Peg was a quiet, well-behaved baby. Of course, most any baby would seem quiet after Chris. She was content to play in the pen and loved it when I gave her horsy back rides around the hard floors. My knees would begin to hurt, but she would dig her little heels into my sides, and I'd be off and quickly crawling again. Once I turned too fast and she went flying off. It was good for her and for me that she landed on her diaper-cushioned butt and not her head, because Mom would have had my head if I hurt little Peg.

When she first learned to walk, she'd roll from side to side, moving in a crooked line. She reminded me of Marty walking home from Rodak's Bar.

Most of the time, little "Peg a Leg" was happy, but when she got mad, her little fists would ball up, her face would turn beet red, and she'd attack me. When she got like this, I knew I had teased her too much.

There were so many of us running around the house now that Mom had trouble keeping names straight. When she wanted Terry, she might call for Pat by accident. We were old enough to know what one of us she meant, but Peg wasn't.

On a hectic day, Mom would often refer to Peg as "what's her name". There were lots of hectic days, so when Peg would come waddling into the kitchen, Mom would say, "There's what's her name?"

Poor Peg!

It must have been very difficult in the Walton home for the kids to keep each others names straight. I think by this time, they now had ten kids. It was hard to know for sure their total number because we didn't hear from them.

More on Grandma Simpson

I can't remember when Dad and I went to Jordan to pick up Grandma Simpson, but I do know that the weather wasn't very cold and it was on a Sunday right after church.

Grandma had her bags by the back door when we got there. She was standing by the porch hugging a lady, and she was crying.

It was a puzzle until Grandma introduced us to the woman

she had been hugging. She was the daughter of the lady Grandma had been looking after.

I thought that the lady at the door was the one Grandma was tending, and Grandma was crying because she hadn't done her job right. I was very wrong. She was crying because the old lady had died.

I was relieved that she had done a good job. I was also seeing a different side to Grandma Simpson. She really cared for the person who had died.

Wonder of wonders!

Now all I had to do was figure out why she didn't like Terry and me.

More on Grandma Quigley

We all knew that Grandma Quigley was failing. She had been getting steadily worse since Grandpa had died.

By now Mom understood Grandma's language. She loved her very much and was saddened to see her failing so quickly.

It was in early summer and Mom was very worried about Grandma Quigley's condition. She told me to ride my bike up to her house and ask Dad how she was doing. She didn't want to call on the phone and disturb anyone in the house.

I parked my bicycle in the front yard and quietly walked into the house. No one was in the kitchen, so I walked through the living room and stood at Grandma's bedroom door. All of my aunts and Uncle Jimmy were standing around her bed and praying. Dad was standing at the foot of the bed, and Doctor Horne was checking Grandma's heart.

It was very quiet and peaceful in the bedroom, except for the sound of soft crying.

Without any warning, Grandma suddenly sat straight up

in bed with her eyes and mouth wide open and limply fell back onto her pillow. It nearly scared me completely to death because I'd never seen Grandma move or look that way.

Doctor Horne checked her heart again and shook his head. My aunts and Uncle Jimmy started to cry. Dad had his back to me, so I couldn't tell if he was crying. He was holding onto the footboard and leaning forward.

Fortunately, no one saw me. I felt like I was spying on them.

I got out of the house as quietly as possible, got on my bike, and pedaled as fast as I could toward home. It's a wonder that I kept from crashing into the ditch because I was crying and my eyes were loaded with tears.

I did notice Mrs. Cashin standing by the road. She could tell by the way I was acting that Grandma was dead and the look on her face showed it.

I got off my bike and ran crying into the house and into Mom's arms. She didn't even ask me what was wrong. We both stood there holding each other and wailing. My brothers and sisters heard the noise and came into the kitchen. They were holding onto Mom and crying because she was crying.

The next day, O'Neill's Funeral Home had Grandma in her Sunday best and in the same spot that Grandpa had been put a bit more than two years earlier.

I was getting used to seeing dead people now, so I didn't mind looking at her.

The bad part came when Aunt Mary told Terry, Pat, John and Mary Kay Calnon, and me that we had to sit in hard chairs in the living room, stay put, and be quiet as mourners came in to pay their final respects.

It was a warm day and the tie I had on didn't help either. The smell of the flowers was sickening. The longer I sat there, the hotter I got. Then, my imagination started playing tricks on me.

I tried very hard not to look at Grandma, but something kept drawing my eyes to her face. I thought I saw her move! I almost messed myself. I kept listening for sounds to come from her when there wasn't anyone but us kids in the room. Any little sound out of the ordinary made me start.

It was a very long three hours, and I never forgave Aunt Mary for making us sit there all that time.

The next morning we all went to St. Bridget's Church for the service and then up to Saint Mary's Cemetery in Skaneateles. Then we all went back to Grandma's house for food and drink. The men didn't drink much because they respected Grandma and knew she wouldn't have wanted them to get tipsy. For them not to drink much when it was good, free whiskey, told me just how great their respect was for her.

The Calnons Leave Stump City

Dad told us a few months after Grandma had died that Uncle Danny, Aunt Pat, and the kids were moving to a place in Florida called Orlando.

I was upset. Terry and Pat were put into a state of shock. Pat was losing her best friend and Terry was losing one of her best friends. They were in sad moods for a long time before they left and a long time after they had gone.

The neighborhood was changing and I didn't like it one bit. Mom said, "Life goes on."

Why did life have to go on this way?

Mom and Michael Make a Curtain

Mom decided that there should be a bit of privacy in our bedroom. How could anyone have privacy with five of us in a room already crammed with three beds and one bunk bed? Heck, the space between each bed was less than a foot now!

Her solution was simple and inexpensive, but not sound-proof. I watched as she measured the distance between the front wall and the wall by the doorway. Next she measured the width of the room on either end and put pencil marks where the room would be divided. She made sure it was close to being in two equal halves.

Armed with a piece of paper with the measurements she needed, she went downstairs with me right behind her. She dug out two very old blankets, went to her Singer sewing machine, and sewed them together after cutting one of them to make it the right length.

The sewing machine was put back in its proper spot in the corner of the living room out of the way of traffic. She left the living room and went straight to the kitchen and out the back door to the tool shed with me, again, right behind her. When we came back, we were armed with heavy duty electric fencing wire, a hand drill, screw driver, wire cutters, a hammer, and two heavy duty eyebolts.

Mom marched upstairs into the bedroom, with me carrying most of the supplies and we started. She took the hammer from me and started to gently tap the wall in the area where she had put the pencil mark. Mom climbed down from the chair she was standing on and told me to drill a hole, right where she had just put another pencil mark. I got up on the chair and started using the drill. First it went through the plaster, and then the lath, and it then turned slowly into a wall stud. I looked down at her and she smiled up at me.

She said, "We've hit pay-dirt, Michael, the bolt won't pull out of the stud."

When I was done drilling, she handed the eyebolt to me, and I started hand-turning the bolt into the wall. When I couldn't turn it anymore, she handed me the long screwdriver, told me to put the end of it into the eyebolt, and turn it until she told me to stop. It went in without too much of a problem, and I stopped when she told me to.

I asked if I could do the tapping on the other wall between the windows. I copied what Mom had done and listened for a solid sound. I heard it and marked the spot with the pencil and did the same things I had done on the other side.

I helped Mom thread the strong wire through the closed loop she had sewn along one edge of the blankets. It took some time because the wire wanted to droop.

This part finished, she got up on the chair and told me to hand the end of the wire to her. I held up the wire and she put the end through the eyebolt and twisted it over the other side of the wire several times with pliers. It was harder for me to hold the other end up because of the added weight of the blankets. Mom put the end of the wire through the other eyebolt and pulled down while I pulled towards her. When the blankets only had a slight bow to them, she cut off the long end, drew the wire as tight as she could with the pliers, and looped it around the wire where it had gone through the eyebolt. Then she repeated the twisting of the wire to secure it.

After she got down and examined the job, she moved the blankets close to the window wall.

I noticed that the other end was short by a good three feet and asked Mom about it.

She said, "That's your entrance way into your side of the room."

I thought that three feet was a bit too wide but didn't say anything.

Now there was a bit of privacy in the room. I could change my underwear without having to turn my back, and Terry and Pat didn't have to go into the other bedroom to get changed. It made things much easier for all of us.

It didn't take me long to figure out a way to scare the girls after they got in bed and settled in a little. I moved the small chair that I used as a clothes rack quietly next to the curtain, stood on it, and stuck my head over the curtain. I wouldn't say anything and wait for one of them to notice. I liked to hear them scream and this worked really well.

I only did it a few times, because Mom threatened to make me scream in pain louder than the girls were screaming with fright.

The Five-Day Vacation Theory, Part VIII

Mom and I had done the curtain job when she looked like she had swallowed a quarter keg of hard cider, and it wasn't long after that she had her old suitcase packed and placed by the bedroom door again.

Peg was in for the same rude awakening that all of us had gone through. Where in the world would she sleep? Would Mom and Dad buy another bunk bed set or put her someplace else in their small room?

It was time for a five-day vacation. Dad loaded Mom into the car while we waved our good-byes from the edge of the road.

Grandma Simpson wasn't working for an old lady at the time, so we were stuck with her.

It sure wasn't a vacation for us. I had to be extra careful with my manners, not tease my brothers and sisters, and stay out of the refrigerator. (Mom and Dad got a used one a few years earlier. The icebox, water tray, and Mr. Weeks were gone.)

I'd given up trying to figure out why the women in the area liked five-day vacations. At the moment Mom was one ahead of Mrs. Tambroni, and she wasn't wearing baggy shirts. This meant that Mom would keep the lead for a while. The Waltons were too far away to know how many were in their family, but I had a feeling Mrs. Walton would still be the smartest woman in the area if she was still around.

Did she lose her title if she was no longer in Stump City? If so, Mom was now the smartest woman in Stump City and even all of Skaneateles Falls.

She didn't act too pleased about being the champ.

Maureen

The usual two days passed and we all climbed into the 1957 Chevy that Dad got from Kennedy Chevrolet earlier in the year. It was brand new when he got it, but was considered a last year's model because it had been sitting on the car lot since last fall. He got a good deal on it, but said the thirty-five-dollar-a-month car payments would put us all in the poor house.

Peg climbed into the front seat and sat between Dad and me. Terry, Pat, John, and Chris piled into the back seat. There was plenty of room because John hadn't grown much and Chris was only four. Besides, Chris couldn't sit still anyway and was standing on the hump and holding onto the front seat while he bounced up and down even before Dad had finished backing out of the driveway.

When we got to the hospital and Dad had parked the car, we all jumped out. The rest of the kids followed me because I knew exactly what floor Mom was on and which wing the baby section was in. Dad followed right behind to make sure the herd stayed together.

We waited for Dad at the visitors' desk so we could check in. After Dad talked to one of the nurses, we followed him to the baby nursery.

It was easy to pick out our new sister because she was the only blond, fair-skinned one in there. She looked like a mixture of Terry and Pat.

Did I really see what I just saw? Impossible! I swear I saw her look over to us and put the tiny back of her hand on her forehead. She even rolled back her eyes a little bit. The movements looked just like the ones I'd seen in very old silent movies when the actress was in distress. It made my head snap back and my jaw fly open when I saw it.

I looked around at my brothers and sisters to see if they had seen it too. None of them seemed to have noticed what she had done. How could they miss it!

After we looked at Maureen for a few more minutes, we made our way down the long hall to Mom's room. She was in a pretty good mood considering what I knew she had gone through. I hadn't told Terry, Pat, or John about what I knew about babies because I didn't know how to explain it without them getting sick or something. It was also very embarrassing for me to talk about.

After we all had given Mom hugs and kisses, she said that the new baby was to be called Maureen, a pretty Irish name. I thought about the name and realized that four of the seven of us had first names starting with "M." I couldn't figure out if it meant anything.

It didn't take us long to shorten Maureen's name to just Mo. So much for the pretty Irish name.

Three days later Mom came home. Terry had the job, when she wasn't in school or given time off, of taking care of Maureen. Pat finished her year plus of a living you-know-what and no longer had to go running around after Chris. She now had Peg to care for when she was around the house. It was like the difference between night and day for her.

Pat didn't smile as much now that she didn't have to take care of Chris. This was a very good thing. I had learned from Mom that the more Pat smiled, the more she was hurting inside. An ear-to-ear smile told Mom that Pat was really sick or in mental trouble.

So far I hadn't changed a single diaper. I was a very lucky boy to escape that miserable job. It was, indeed, a man's world, and I loved it.

Peg's New Bed

Peg knew what was coming but wasn't ready for what was waiting for her in our bedroom. Mom and Dad hadn't bought another bunk bed set nor had they put a bed in their room. Peg's bed was to be the top of the old steamer trunk right at the end of the curtain. Now I knew why Mom had made the entrance to our side of the room wide.

Mom put several old, thick blankets on top of the trunk to make a mattress and had cut and sewn old sheets to make them fit the blankets.

I tried it out. It wasn't very comfortable.

Peg didn't complain. She just looked at me when she saw where she was going to sleep, raised her hands palms up by her head, shrugged her shoulders, and lifted her eyebrows. All of it together said, "What did you expect?"

She'd wake up in the morning and have two marks on her back or side, depending how she had last slept before waking, from the support ribs that ran over the top of the trunk. She never said anything about sleeping on top of the trunk.

I don't ever remember her falling off the trunk. If she had and I had seen it, she probably would have given me the same gesture she gave me when she found out the old steamer trunk was her bed.

What a trooper!

The Waltons Return to Stump City

Just before school started, Stump City got back to being almost normal again. Without warning, the Waltons suddenly returned from Arizona. It took them all a few days to get over being in the car like sardines in a can on their long trip back. Even Grandpa Walton returned from Mexico, New York, to make the family complete.

Mr. Walton either decided that it was not all that great there, or Mrs. Walton and the kids talked him into coming back.

Davy never told me why, and I didn't ask. It was enough that he and the family had returned to give back Stump City the spirit and noise it had been missing since they left.

Mrs. Walton now had ten kids. She took back the championship from Mom, and Mom didn't seem to mind because she didn't look at all unhappy about it.

Our big, used clothes center was back too.

The Arrival of the Television

The major event of the year, and most any year, happened. Dad came home with a black and white television! We watched as he plugged the television into different outlets in the living room. He was looking for the best spot to pull in the signals from the two television stations in Syracuse. When he found the best spot, he placed it on a small table. The picture wasn't that great, but none of us minded. It quickly replaced the radio as our major source of entertainment.

Mom soon found out that Chris would sit and watch it and stay out of trouble. The television was on a lot.

My favorite shows were: *Roy Rogers and Dale Evans, The Lone Ranger, The Buster Brown Show, Pinky Lee,* and *Lassie.*

Mom and Dad always watched *Gun Smoke* on Saturday nights. If we had behaved the day it was on, we older ones could stay up and watch it. I didn't miss many episodes because I tried my hardest to be good on Saturdays.

At seven o'clock every Sunday night, the whole family would sit down and watch *Disneyland.* Mom would give a five cent candy bar to each of us old enough to chew on one. The candy bar was our one big treat of the week.

We all went into a mild case of depression when the television went "on the blink". Mr. Garafelo was the area T.V. repairman. He was very busy because tubes had to be replaced often in televisions.

When he finally found the time to get to our house, we'd all hold our breath and hope he had the right tube in his case. If he did, we'd start breathing again at a normal pace. If he didn't, and he had to take the set with him, it was like a family member being taken to the hospital for emergency surgery. If this was the case, the T.V. would be gone for a week or so and we'd go back to listening to the radio.

Mom would be the saddest because it meant Chris would be on the run again, and the noise level in the house would increase because the rest of us would no longer be silent like we would be while watching a show.

Life went painfully on without the T.V. in the house.

Pinky Lee

I can't remember what year it was when it happened, but it scared me. I was watching The *Pinky Lee* show. Pinky was doing his usual tap dancing and singing.

Without warning, he put both hands on his heart and said, "Oh, my goodness."

He fell to the floor and the picture went black.

I knew something bad had happened.

On the news that night, a man said that Pinky Lee had suffered a heart attack.

I prayed for Pinky because I knew, from what happened to Grandpa Quigley, that a heart attack could kill a person.

I don't know how long it was before Pinky was back on the television, but he did come back.

My prayers had been answered.

Michael Starts Sixth Grade

It was time for Terry, Pat, John, and me to start school. I was going into the sixth grade.

I had heard that it was better to have Mr. Sackett. Kids

were telling me that if I got Miss Wallace, I would be dead before Christmas.

I wanted to have Mr. Sackett. I had never had a man teacher. I wanted to see if there was a difference between the way a man and woman teacher handled a class. Plus, I wanted to live until Christmas.

I found out that I had Miss Wallace. Now I knew I wouldn't see another Christmas.

All of Miss Wallace's students, myself included, were scared to enter her room on the first day. We finally had to go in because the school bell rang. I buried myself into the middle of the flock of sheep being led to slaughter and hunched down because I was taller than most of the other kids. We were all so close together that it's a wonder we didn't trip over each other and make a big pile of petrified kids right in front of her.

After attendance was taken, she told us to go to the desk she would be standing next to when she called our names. She did it by our last names. Wouldn't you know it! I drew the front seat in the third row. It was right in front of her big oak desk.

I didn't look to either side or make a move. I looked straight ahead at her desk while she completed assigning seats to the rest of the students.

To my horror, she had a ruler on the corner of her desk just like Sister used in Church School. This wasn't looking good at all.

When we were settled into our assigned seats, she started handing out textbooks and covers. She explained very carefully how to put them on and told us how to label each book.

I paid very close attention. I didn't want to feel that ruler. She looked much tougher than Sister and the blow would surely break a knuckle or two.

The only noise I heard while we were doing the book covers was the sound of paper being creased and folded.

No one had made a mistake, and she seemed pleased with us. She smiled. Was it an evil smile or a good smile? I couldn't tell.

The task done and inspected, she told us to place the books inside our desks in a certain order. She said the order of the books was the order in which she taught the subjects.

Miss Wallace was making a lot of sense. Is there such a thing as a madwoman who made sense?

She told us to be very careful with the books because they were very expensive. She suggested that we treat each one as if it was the Holy Book.

That made sense too because we now knew how important the textbooks were to her.

I was beginning to get worried. When was she going to turn into a madwoman?

Poor Cathy Mitchell made the mistake of dropping one of Miss Wallace's Holy Books onto the floor.

We all stopped breathing. Cathy Mitchell did too, and she also looked like she was about to wet herself.

Miss Wallace looked at her and said, "Cathy, please be more careful with the books. I know the desktops are slippery because they are freshly cleaned and waxed."

What was going on here? I was beginning to sweat because the kids on the bus were usually on the mark when they said something about a teacher.

The only time I remember the bus being wrong was when it was spread around that Miss MacKaig had died. That was an easy one to believe because Miss MacKaig made dirt look like new when I had her. It turned out that she had not died. It was her pet cat that had gone down, and Miss MacKaig was so heartbroken that she just couldn't be in school for a day. When I heard that news, I felt sorry for Miss MacKaig because the cat was probably her best friend.

Nothing happened during science or English. Miss Wallace was teaching in a way that even I could understand.

She took us outside for playground after English. She stood silently by one of the swing supports and watched us play.

I didn't get to ask anyone about what was going on with Miss Wallace because I wasn't that far away from her. I did this with purpose because I liked to just get close enough to a possible danger to judge it better. I could see some students who were behind her talking to each other and keeping an eye on Miss Wallace at the same time. They all had puzzled looks on their faces.

We got back to the classroom in good order and quickly when she told us that our playground time was over.

She told us to take out our math books. It was easy for us to do because they were right on top of the other books.

Miss Wallace wanted us to review different shapes to take some of the rust off after being away from school for the summer. She then picked up a piece of chalk and reached for the ruler on top of her desk.

The moment had finally come. Now we would see the real Miss Wallace. I could imagine her changing from a nice lady who made lots of sense into a bigger and meaner Sister.

She turned around and drew a hexagon on the board using the ruler as a straight edge. The air came out of my lungs and I could breathe again. I could hear the same sound of air escaping in different parts of the room. The kids making the sound were the same ones who had the Church School class with me.

We talked about Miss Wallace during lunchtime. Everyone agreed that the bus was wrong. We started to relax a bit.

The rest of the day went great. We learned that it was okay to wiggle a bit in our seats, to drum our pencils on desktops, to rustle paper in a polite way, to smile once in a while, and even to laugh when something funny happened.

Most of us liked Miss Wallace. As the weeks passed, we began to know how far we could go without getting a certain look. The look was one of disappointment. If I got one, and I got more than my share, it seemed to hurt to my very soul.

Don't get me wrong, she still would yell at me or another student, but she only did so when we started acting too much like boys and the classroom was starting to act more like the playground.

I think the bus wasn't wrong. The bus just didn't know how to put into words something that hurt more than Sister's ruler: Miss Wallace's look of disapproval.

Mary Cotter

For some strange reason, I started looking at a girl in class in a different way. Her name was Mary Cotter. She was new to the school. Mary's dark, beautiful, well-combed hair, bright smile, sparkling eyes, and spring in her step made me look at her like I had never looked at a girl before. It also helped that Miss Wallace seemed to like Mary more than the other girls in class. If Miss Wallace thought she was special, then I did too.

It was hard to sneak a look because she sat back a few seats from me and over to my right. It was grand when Miss Wallace asked her a question. It gave me a legal excuse to turn around. I didn't hear what she said. I just looked at her while I listened to her voice. That was enough to put me into a trance for the rest of the period.

When playground time came around, I would do whatever I was doing with only half of my mind thinking about what I was playing because I would be constantly looking in Mary's direction as if I were trying to find a friend. If she looked anywhere in my direction, I'd turn away so she wouldn't know I was looking at her.

I knew she could never like me. The other kids had teased me for years about my bright orange-red hair and freckles. I was called "Carrot Top" or "Barney Google" when the kids got into a teasing jag, which was often. The freckles would fade just a bit during the winter but blossom in the spring, when the sun got stronger, like the flowers in our neighbor Mrs. Wickham's garden.

I believed I was a mess. To add to my own feelings about myself, one time the gym teacher got after me to run faster by yelling, "Move that tub of fat, Quigley!"

His words got the gym class laughing. Heck, I couldn't even do one pull-up in class because my weight was too much for me to lift. I understood why many of the other kids couldn't do one, but I was stronger than most of the kids in the class and should be able to do at least one.

Rich was teased a lot too. We became even closer friends. We were comrades in arms because of our common suffering.

Mary would smile and say hello to me, but I knew she was just being polite.

The Arrival of the Gas Furnace

When I got home from school one day, a large crew of men was digging a trench along the side of the road. They were already close to Mr. McEneny's house.

I found out from Dad that a gas line was going to be put in to the end of our street. The line was already done along Jordan Road, and most of the homes in Skaneateles Falls had already gone from using coal for heat to natural gas.

It didn't take the men more than three days to get the line run to the end of our street and pipes running right to the basement of every house.

Dad decided that a gas furnace would be cheaper, safer, and easier to run than the old coal stove.

Before a furnace could be installed, Dad needed to build a chimney on the outside of the house. He decided that the best spot was next to the kitchen window.

He got in touch with Mr. Finney, a friend and a mason, and they started the job.

I watched them lay the blocks and put the clay flue inside. Dad showed me how to mix the mortar in the wheelbarrow and let me try. It was even better than fixing a cake mix with Mom because I could be a little sloppy about doing it. The only downside was not being able to lick out the bowl.

After two days of work, Dad and Mr. Finney were almost done and well above the roof line.

I decided I wanted to get a closer look, so I carefully climbed up the ladder. I got as far as a rung near the top of the ladder and stopped to watch them work.

After a minute or two, Dad turned around. When he saw me, his eyes got really big. He said in a calm voice, "Son, climb down the ladder real slow."

I did what Dad said to do. I looked up once to see Dad and Mr. Finney looking down at me. He and the mason both watched me climb down. When I got to the bottom and looked back up at them again, they both looked relieved.

After Dad knew I was safe, he said in a very harsh voice,

"Michael, stay away from the ladder. If I see you anywhere near it, I'm coming down and tan your hide!"

I was puzzled and hurt for a few minutes before I understood. I had put a great fear in Dad and Mr. Finney when they saw me so high off the ground.

Not long after the chimney was done, Mr. Manley came over to install the furnace. Dad helped him carry it into the basement and get it placed in the right spot.

The furnace came in a huge cardboard box.

I got an idea and asked Dad if I could have it.

After he found out what I was going to do with it, he gave it to me.

I took the box out back and asked Mom for a knife. I cut a small window into one side of the box.

It was hard to handle the big box, but I somehow managed to get it to the top of our snow covered hill. I faced the side of the box where I had cut the hole downhill, carefully climbed inside, and took off. It picked up speed quickly and I made it to the bottom. My idea had worked!

I went to the back door and yelled for my brothers and sisters to come out and try it.

We all had a great time going down the hill in the box. It lasted for at least five runs before it came apart. Then I ripped big pieces from it, and we went down on them. If we hit a little bump, we'd go flying off the cardboard in long, fast rolls.

Peg went the fastest because she was the lightest. Her red pigtails would be flopping up and down and act like small bullwhips when she took a tumble. She'd get up laughing, run up the hill, and go down over and over again.

It was great fun while it lasted.

Thanksgiving 1958

We had our first Thanksgiving at home. It sure was strange not to be going to Uncle Danny's and Aunt Pat's house. We had a good time at home, but, oh, we missed the Calnons and our Grandma and Grandpa Quigley.

I felt sorry for Dad because he no longer had a live parent.

I didn't like to think about Mom and Dad being dead.

Christmas 1958

Just before Christmas came, I had one of the biggest shocks of my life. Mom sent me down to the cellar to fetch up some potatoes for supper. After I filled the bucket about a third full (we ate lots and lots of spuds) I turned to go back up the stairs. Something caught my attention. I looked up to the ceiling and noticed a long box.

I quietly took it down to see what it was. It was a Daisy Red Rider BB gun! It was the exact model that I had written down on a piece of paper and sent up in smoke to Santa.

I was stunned, shocked, and crushed. There was no Santa Claus after all.

The kids on the bus were right!

What a fool I'd been. I was going on thirteen and I should have known better.

I put the gun box back on the rafter and slowly went upstairs.

On Christmas Day I knew what I was getting. I tried to act surprised when I tore the wrapping paper off the box, but felt like I'd pulled it off badly.

I pretended to believe in Santa because I didn't want my

brothers and sisters to go through the same disappointment that I was having.

At least I didn't have to be afraid anymore about Santa suddenly appearing in our bedroom on Christmas Eve.

Santa went up in smoke.

I loved the BB gun and would shoot at almost anything. The sparrows around the house were thinned out. Bullet, the O'Hara boys' very vicious dog, started giving me plenty of room when he saw me carrying the gun. He stayed out of range when he saw me with it because I'd shot him in the butt a few times to get even with him for all the fear he gave me when I was younger. I got so good at shooting it that I could even hit the electric fence wiring that went around Rocky's pasture from about thirty feet away.

Michael's Sixth Grade Trip

Just before school got out for summer vacation, our class started getting all excited about our class trip to Albany. It was a big sign that we were getting on in years because up to this point our class trips had been to local parks and museums.

It didn't take me long to realize that it would be grand to see Mary somewhere other than school. She lived right in Elbridge close to the school and had a two-minute walk home. I wished that she and her family would move to Stump City.

The only drawback to the trip was riding on the yellow thing with six wheels. Just the thought of the 150 mile ride to Albany made cold sweat beads break out on my freckled forehead. It was only three miles on the bus to school. How would I survive a trip to Albany? I prayed hard about it after we said our normal prayers at bedtime.

It wasn't hot on the day of the trip. I was worried about the heat because heat and bus didn't mix well in my stomach.

Just a few minutes before we were to board the bus Miss Wallace said, "Make sure you go before we leave. The bus is not going to stop until we get to the museum in Albany." Her very slow, serious tone of voice and the way she looked when she said it, told us that she really and truly would not let the bus stop at any rest areas.

Most of us immediately asked for permission to go to the bathroom.

After we got our business done, we all got on the bus. Miss Wallace and the girls sat in front. All of us boys sat toward the back with Mr. Sackett, the other sixth grade teacher.

I don't remember much about the ride there because most of the time I was looking at Mary and not out the window. I'd mumble a word or two to Rich when he said something just to be polite.

About and hour into the trip, several of the kids were squirming in their seats. Every time we passed a rest area, I could see a look of great pain come to their faces.

The kid who had the hardest time on the way to Albany was Little Eddie. He sat one seat ahead and just across the aisle from me. We were not even close to Syracuse when he started squirming. Shortly after, he stopped squirming. Had he wet himself? No, because a bit after, he started squirming again. It wasn't long after that he started moving his legs back and forth. At first it was in slow motion; then it turned into a full knee-banging affair. By the time we passed a sign that said "Amsterdam Next Exit," he went to the highest level. He was actually holding his crotch in public like a kindergarten kid. This was very serious. I thought he'd cry next to get rid of some of the water, but he didn't.

When Miss Wallace stood up and told us that we would be at the museum in a few minutes, Little Eddie was standing up and dancing from one foot to the other. Miss Wallace knew what was going on and showed great mercy by not telling Little Eddie to sit down.

As soon as the bus stopped in front of the museum, Miss Wallace took Little Eddie and other kids in physical pain—more than half the busload—to the bathroom while the rest of us followed behind with Mr. Sackett in charge.

We waited for the kids already in the bathroom to get out before we went in. Little Eddie was the last one out from the first round of visitors. He seemed to be limp with relief and had a sheepish look on his face. I didn't see a wet spot on his pants. Eddie was a fighter.

On the trip I kept waiting for the sick feeling to start in my stomach, but it never did. My concentrating on Mary Cotter made the three-hour trip fly by—a lot faster than it did for Eddie.

My prayer had been half answered. I'd pray some more before we left to go back home.

The museum tour went well. The rest of the class learned about the way Indians lived, saw Revolutionary War things, and even saw a woolly mammoth. I did stop looking at Mary long enough to gaze in awe at the hairy, giant creature.

During the middle of the tour, we all went outside to a nice park to eat lunch. Mom had packed peanut butter and jelly sandwiches for me and threw in a few cookies for dessert. I was starved by this time because it was much later than our normal lunch period in school.

I couldn't see Mary, so I dug into my lunch. I had a good time talking to Dave Morgan, another friend, and Rich. It felt good to be back in a man's world for a bit of time.

After we finished the tour, Miss Wallace told us to go to the bathroom because it was a long ride home and we wouldn't be stopping. Little Eddie was the first one in.

Eddie had been a good example for all of us because on the way back nobody even squirmed.

About half-way home, I noticed that the girls around Mary were in a serious discussion. Mary didn't have the usual happy expression on her face.

By the time we had returned to the bus circle in front of the school, Mary was about to burst into tears.

I was very worried about her.

All of the town kids got off the bus and began to walk home. By the time Mary got to the sidewalk in front of the school, she was crying hard.

I hadn't felt this bad about someone since the time Bobby Kulle, who lived next to the Waltons, took a nasty fall down the side of the quarry dump and cut his head wide open.

On the bus ride home, I was in pain for Mary.

I never did find out what caused her to cry.

I was learning that girls are much worse than boys when it comes to being mean with words. They can have very nasty tongues.

Mary was the focus of my school year, and my grades suffered because of it. I'd try to concentrate on schoolwork, but it was very hard.

Miss Wallace made several phone calls home and sent many notes home with me. The calls and the notes helped me a bit.

I was very nervous about getting my report card.

When I did get it and showed it to Mom, she seemed to relax. I knew then that I had passed.

I would be going into seventh grade, the grade where we started going to different rooms for all our classes.

Would I see Mary? Would she be in any of my classes? I sure hoped so.

The Waltons Leave Stump City Again

In the spring, Stump City got some bad news. The Waltons were moving to a bigger house close to Skaneateles Lake in Mandana.

I asked Dad where Mandana was. He told me that it was about six miles down the lake on the west side.

It wasn't good that they were moving, but Mandanna wasn't nearly as far away as Arizona. Maybe I'd get to see Davy once in a while.

Life in Stump City would soon be drained down a few notches again.

Swimming in Jordan Pool

Since the end of third grade, my first time through, I'd been taking the school bus to Jordan Pool during the summer. I went three times a week for a few hours in the morning.

It was great. First I would drop off my change of clothes in the locker room and then go to lessons. I started in the shallow end, learning how to breathe from side to side, doing the doggy paddle, and sticking my head under water. After the lesson, the swim class was allowed to go down the huge water slides and play in the shallow area.

Every summer I would learn more advanced swimming strokes and was becoming a decent swimmer

After four or five years in the swim program, most of the students who went on a regular basis graduated to the "deep end." I longed, since I started lessons, to be good enough to swim on the "deep end" side of the rope that divided beginners from more advanced swimmers.

Now that I had graduated, I was nervous to jump in. The shallow part of the "deep end" was over my head, and the deepest part by the high diving board was twelve feet deep. When we went in for the first time, none of us sank to the bottom, a great relief for all of us.

We practiced different strokes to get better at them and learned some of the basic life-saving skills.

I liked swimming, so I paid very close attention to what the swim instructors had to say.

Playtime in the "deep end" wasn't as much fun as it was in the "shallow end" because we couldn't touch bottom. I'd practice going off the small diving board and doing a good dive.

The day came when our instructor told us we were going to be jumping off the high diving board. It was at least ten feet above the water.

The instructor told us it was hard to go off it for the first time, but after that, it would become easier. She warned us that if we did a belly smacker, we would suffer greatly. She then slowly told us all the proper steps to use while jumping off the board. After she had gone through the steps again, she climbed to the top and did exactly what she had told us to do. She made the jump look very easy and landed in the water without making much of a splash.

When the instructor got out of the water, she told us to form a single line. I was in the middle.

During the pause after a kid had jumped off and swam far enough away so it was safe for the next kid to go, I kept going over what the swim instructor had told us: hold our noses with one hand, take a deep breath, jump out a little from the board, and keep our feet together.

Timmy was two kids ahead of me. He was acting brave.

When he got to the end of the board, he held his nose, jumped out a little, and had his legs spread wide apart.

It took Timmy a long time to come up because he was only using one hand. The other one was holding his private parts. The look on his face was terrible to see. His mouth was wide open and his eyes were tightly shut. After he slowly got out of the pool (it's hard to do using one hand) he ran to the locker room and stayed there until it was time to get on the bus to go home.

When I got to the end of the board, I stopped for a moment to look down. It was higher up than the bedroom window at home! I knew I had to jump off. The boy who was supposed to go after Timmy had gotten out of line and went to sit on the lifeguard bench behind the board. The girls looked at him as if he was some kind of coward—I didn't want to get the same look.

I thought of the look and also the proper way of jumping off the board and let myself go. It felt like I did it to perfection. The lifeguard didn't think the same. She said that I should relax my legs a little.

I didn't say anything to her but I was thinking, "Are you kidding me? Didn't you see what happened to poor Timmy?"

Growing Pains

The summer turned into a time of pain. About three months before summer, I started to wake up once in a while during the night. All my joints hurt. I got used to it and was able to sleep through most nights. Now I'd lie awake hurting and couldn't go back to sleep.

I finally asked Mom about it. She took out the yardstick,

told me to stand against the wall where she measured all of us, and measured me.

Mom said, "You've grown three inches since your birthday. No wonder you have been hurting."

She looked me up and down and told me to stand directly in front of her. I could almost look her directly in the eyes!

She said, "It won't be long before you're taller. Just don't get too big for your britches. If you do, I'll knock you down a peg or two."

I knew she meant it.

Mowing—Part III

In late spring, Dad got a used Reo gas-powered reel mower like the one Mr. McEneny had bought several years ago. Rose would mow their big lawn twice as fast as I could mow our smaller lawn.

I had wanted Dad to get one since the McEnenys got theirs, but he always came up with the usual "We can't afford it."

Dad showed me how to fill it with gas, check the oil, and start it. Once it was running, he showed me how to put it in and out of gear. He told me not to give it much gas until I got used to it. It wasn't long before I was at a trot behind it.

Its two wheels pulled the machine across the lawn. All I had to do was to steer it and keep my feet away from the blades.

One day Mr. Kimak, who lived at the end of the street, was driving by our house. He saw me mowing and stopped to talk to me. He asked me if I would be willing to mow his lawn. He'd pay me a dollar and a quarter if I did.

I told him that I had to ask Dad first and would let him know if Dad would let me.

At the time, what Mr. Kimak wanted to pay me was five

times more than I was making doing chores around the house and mowing our lawn. It was a huge sum of money. I would even be able to buy a snack at the Jordan Pool snack stand like most of the other kids did.

I waited for Dad to get home from work, get himself changed, and talk to Mom a bit. I had learned to let him get into the house and relax a little before asking him about anything important.

He said that I could, but I would have to give him ten cents for the gas I used and for the wear and tear on the mower.

I was thrilled. It was my first real job.

I went down to talk to Mr. Kimak. He showed me where to mow and places where stones stuck a bit out of the ground. I had to go around them because the stones would ruin the blade on the mower.

The next morning I got the mower out of the tool shed, fired it up, and went down to Mr. Kimak's. His house was the last one on the street and next to Mr. Bennett's home.

The lawn was big and took me at least an hour to mow. Mr. Kimak came out when I was done and examined the lawn. He smiled and gave me a dollar bill and a quarter. I was a very happy working man.

I went home and showed Mom the money I earned.

She was happy and said, "Now you can start paying me some money for clothes and pay for your milk at school next year."

I knew a cartoon of milk cost two cents, so that wasn't a big deal, but I wasn't sure how much the clothes would cost.

I decided that one snack a week at the pool would have to be enough. Besides, I had dreamed about having a new bike for a long time. The bike I rode was used by at least two other boys before I got it and wasn't in very good condition.

It would take a lot of mowing to pay for clothes and milk and have enough left over to save up for a brand new bike, a big dream.

Not long after I started mowing Mr. Kimak's lawn once a week, Mr. Phillips, who lived on the southern fringe of Stump City, stopped by and asked if I'd like to mow his lawn. He asked me to come to his place with him to check it out.

It was a pretty small lawn. The only hard parts about mowing it were the side hill next to a field and going around Mrs. Phillip's flower gardens. He told me that he would pay me a dollar to mow it. A dollar! It was less than half the size of Mr. Kimak's lawn and he wanted to pay me a dollar! To top it off, Mrs. Phillips said she would always have a cookie and a small glass of milk waiting for me when I finished mowing.

I was going to get what Dad called a "fringe benefit."

I told Mr. Phillips that I would have to ask Dad first.

Dad said that I could, but I would have to pay him five cents for each time I mowed it.

I was learning quickly about "business expenses."

Counting my allowance, I would now be making two dollars and fifty cents a week. It was a good, steady income.

I asked Mom how much school clothes would cost me for the year. She thought a moment and decided it would only be about ten dollars because Mrs. Walton told her I could have the old clothes Davy had outgrown.

I sure was glad that Davy was still growing and still bigger than me.

When I had earned enough money to pay for my clothes, I gave it to Mom, and she put it in a jar. I then set aside enough money for milk for the school year, about four dollars, forty cents for snacks at the pool, and another five dollars to buy a

Nutty Buddy ice cream bar or ice cream sandwich once a week at the school cafeteria.

I was learning how to handle large sums of money.

Errands of Mercy

Towards the middle of summer, as I was walking by Big Jim McEneny's house, he called me over to his side lawn. He was pretty old by now. During the heat of the day, he liked to sit in the shade of a big maple tree that overhung from his neighbor's side of the property line.

He was wondering if I'd like to make a trip to Cronaeur's General Store once in a while to pick up things he needed. He said that he would pay me for my effort.

I told him that I'd do it for nothing, but he was determined to pay me.

I agreed to go to the store for him.

Big Jim told me to stay in the shade while he went into his house. He came back out a few minutes later with a grocery list held in his massive hand and told me to look it over.

The first item on the list was a quart of Genesee beer. The rest of the list had the usual items purchased at the store: a half pound of store cheese, a loaf of bread, and a quarter pound of sliced ham.

I told him I understood what he wanted and wouldn't be gone long.

He said, "Make it quick, Michael me boy. A man could die of the thirst on a hot day like this."

I thought about going home first to ask Mom if she needed anything from the store, but I could tell Big Jim had a powerful need for The Drink.

It only took about ten minutes to walk to Cronaeur's store going the long, safe way, but I decided to please Big Jim by cutting off a good four minutes by taking the short cut through the woods that had the community dump in it. The trail went past the dump, over a wooden foot bridge, behind the Waterbury Felt Company building, and up the railroad tracks.

The tricky part was the foot bridge that was placed over a constantly muddy area. It never got much sunlight, was always slippery, and went up and down as someone walked across it.

I didn't even take the time to look around when I went inside the store, which was very hard for me to do. Instead, I walked right up to the counter, said hello to Mr. Cronaeur and handed him the list. I quickly walked back to the huge cooler and pulled out a quart bottle of Genesee beer. With the big bottle of beer in one hand, I grabbed a loaf of bread off the bread shelf on my way back to the counter.

I stood and waited patiently for Mr. Cronaeur to slice the cheese from the big cheese wheel on the counter and slice up the ham at the meat counter. He wrapped the ham and cheese, carefully placed the beer in a separate bag and put it in the bottom of another bag before packing the cheese, sliced ham, and the bread around the bottle.

I asked him to put it on Big Jim's tab, thanked him, and said good-bye.

I didn't even take the time to stick around long enough to get a piece of penny candy, which I knew he would give me.

I hurried on back and slowed down only when I got to the foot bridge. I was very careful there.

I didn't mind if I fell in the mud, but if I fell and broke the big bottle of beer, I might as well have dropped Holy Communion out of my mouth and onto the floor in church.

I breathed easier when I made it across with the Holy Drink still in one piece and quickened my pace.

Big Jim acted surprised when he saw me.

He said, "Good boy, Michael. The devil himself must've been on your tail to make it back so quickly." He added, "Good job, Michael, good job," as he popped the top off the bottle with an opener he had pulled from his back pocket.

After he took a deep pull from the bottle, he slowly reached into a front pocket. This time he pulled out some change and handed me a fifty-cent piece.

I told him it was too much for such an easy job.

Big Jim said, "Nonsense, me boy. 'Twas a job well done. Now be gone with you, and leave me beside meself while I rest me old bones in comfort."

I thanked him and waved back to him as I took off down the road headed for home.

I burst into the kitchen to show Mom the money and tell her how I got it.

She said, "Your father has told me from time to time that Big Jim is well-heeled, but you'd never know it by looking at him."

I went upstairs and counted all my money. I was almost half-way to getting the new bike. I had saved fifteen dollars.

I made it a daily habit to walk by Big Jim's house. I soon learned that the hot days when he'd be sitting in the shade were the best ones for having to make a trip for him to Cronaeur's store. The quart bottle of Genesee beer would always be at the top of his list.

I'd go to bed praying for hot days, even though we'd all suffer from the heat that same night. We had lots of hot days that summer, and Big Jim McEneny drank lots of Genesee.

A New Bicycle

Meltzner's Bike Store in Syracuse ran an ad at least once a week in the *Post Standard*. I'd look at the wonderful pictures of bikes and dream about having a new bike. I was getting very anxious and excited about buying one.

Toward the end of summer, I had saved enough money to buy one. The one I wanted was thirty-five dollars, a small fortune. It had a light in front, pedal brakes, and an enclosed support bar around the one that went between the legs.

Dad said that he would take me in to Syracuse when he had to go there to get something, which wasn't very often.

A week passed and then another. I bit my tongue, because it didn't pay to pester Dad.

During supper one evening, Dad finally told me that he had to go into Syracuse to buy a new part for Mom's stove. We would go the next day when he got home from work.

The next day dragged on very slowly after I got home from Jordan Pool with Terry and Pat.

When Dad finally got home, it seemed to take hours before we finally climbed into the car.

Dad drove to the parts store first. The man behind the counter was having a hard time finding the part because our stove was so old. I stood there moving my weight from one foot to the other. I tried to kill time by looking out the window at people and cars going by the store. It seemed to take the man a day or so before he at last found the right part.

When we pulled up in front of Meltzner's Bike Store, I couldn't believe the size of the place and the number of new bikes parked on the sidewalk. I was in Boy Heaven.

A salesman came up and asked if he could help. Dad looked down at me in a way that told me that I was in charge, so I looked at the salesman and told him exactly what I was looking for.

He led us into the store and to the bike I had described.

It was absolutely beautiful. It had a different kind of beauty than the kind Mary Cotter had.

There were several different colors. I narrowed the colors down to red and blue and decided that red was better.

We went out to the sidewalk where I was allowed to test ride the bike. It pedaled easily and didn't make any rubbing noises or wobble like my old one did. I was smiling from ear to ear by the time I turned around and headed back to the front of the store.

I got off the bike, put the kickstand down, and we walked back into the store.

The salesman went behind the counter and said, "That will be thirty-five dollars."

I reached into my pocket and pulled out the well-worn billfold that Dad had given me a few years back after he got a new one, and I began counting out my money. It was all one-dollar bills. When I had reached twenty-three and was out of paper money, I pulled out the change that was weighing down my pants and counted out the twelve dollars needed to close the deal.

The salesman handed me a piece of paper marked with the amount I had paid. He told me that if I had any problems with the bike to just bring it back and it would be fixed at no charge.

I held the trunk lid open wide while Dad carefully placed the bike inside. He couldn't quite get the bike all the way in, so he took a piece of string from the trunk and tied the lid down tightly across the rubber tire that stuck out. He didn't want to put any scratches on the paint. Dad knew how important the bike was to me.

My brothers, sisters, and Mom hurried out of the house to look at the bike. I was very happy to go over all of its details with them. I got on it and rode it up and down the street a few times to get used to it.

Mom asked if she could try it. She got on and took a short spin. I think she would have liked to ride on it longer, but her skirt was getting in the way.

I wouldn't let Terry ride it. I was afraid she'd run it into something. I would have to kill her if she scratched it up.

I rode the bike all over the place and became a local speed demon.

Now I could keep up with my friends when we went riding, and it was nice to know I could go faster than most of them when I wanted. I didn't speed ahead very often because I knew what it was like to struggle just to keep close to the back of the pack of bikes.

With mowing lawns, going to the pool three times a week, riding my bicycle, and thinking about Mary Cotter once in a while, the summer flew by.

I noticed that my "baby" fat was melting away, and I was now taller than Mom.

Life was, oh, so good—especially when Dad didn't go to Murray's Bar.

The Seventh Grade

Toward the end of August, I worried about going from class to class, getting lost, going to the wrong room, and not seeing Mary Cotter. I was anxious to get started, but not wanting to start at the same time.

When it did start and I got my class schedule in homeroom, I found myself taking more than one deep breath. I didn't want to make a mess out of my first day in seventh grade.

I didn't go to the wrong classroom, I didn't get lost in the halls, and I didn't see Mary Cotter.

I kept looking for her. In the afternoon just before we had to get on the buses, I got up the nerve to ask one of her girlfriends where she was. She told me that Mary had moved to somewhere near Skaneateles and was going to school there.

She was only a few miles down the road, but she might as well have been in Arizona. I felt a deep emptiness inside.

It didn't take me long to decide that I liked shop class, American history, and science the best.

Miss MacDonald was the shop teacher. She knew even more than Mom about doing things with wood. She spoke in a very slow, no-nonsense tone. I think she did this for a good reason: She had been teaching for many years and knew if boys didn't understand the importance of safety, some of them would lose body parts in her class.

Before she would let us use any power tool for the first time, she would go over and over again the position of our hands, how to hold the wood, and the correct angles for cutting and drilling.

During the school year, we made many nice wood projects for gifts and Christmas presents.

No one got any serious cuts in our class, but a boy in high school who seemed to be in the principal's office at least once a week, had to go to the hospital. He hadn't listened to Miss MacDonald about the proper use of a wood planer and smoothed out the ends of a few fingers.

Miss MacDonald told us all the gory details in class the next day in her very slow way. She had a slight smile on her face when she spoke as if to say, "See, this is what can happen if you don't listen."

By her tone, I could tell that she was a bit pleased that the boy who got hurt was the one who had caused her so much trouble and had had more than one close call with a power tool.

When she was done, she told us to go to our stations.

As I walked by the planer, I looked for blood spots and skin. I didn't see any.

Miss MacDonald kept a very neat shop room, and she probably had the mess cleaned up before the boy got out of the building and loaded into the nurse's station wagon.

Mr. Reagan wasn't much taller than I was, and I outweighed him by a few pounds, but his presence in class was powerful. The word had gotten out that he was a Marine WWII veteran who fought in the Pacific, so I knew before going into his classroom for the first time to be respectful.

He taught us American history in a straight-forward manner. He didn't stay behind his desk much. He'd quickly cruise up and down the aisles with his back very straight, and make military marching turns when he got to the end of one row and went down another one.

Once in a while he'd get off-course and talk about the War. It was fascinating to listen to him. He'd stand still and get a far-away look in his eyes before he began to speak. He told us about being shot at by snipers hidden in coconut trees, being strafed by Zeros, and Japanese soldiers charging at him who didn't care if they lived or died.

I think he survived all the battles on the Japanese held islands because he was short, smart, and quick.

The science teacher, Mr. Marks, was my favorite. He had a square jaw, big arm muscles, walked as if he had big springs in his legs, and spoke in a deep soft voice.

If some boy got a little out of hand, all he had to do was look at him and the culprit would know he had gone too far.

I never got one of his looks because I didn't want to disappoint him.

When a class left his room and our class entered, I'd check to see if he had his safety glasses around his neck. If he did, I knew he was going to do an experiment for us.

He would make a big show of it when he did. The best ones always involved a Bunsen burner, matches, and chemicals. Things would go up in clouds of smoke or make loud noises.

No, gym wasn't one of my favorite classes. I was still a little chubby, freckled, and red haired. The mix of the three seemed to draw Coach's eyes on me. I wasn't the fastest kid and had trouble getting even half-way up the rope. He constantly told me that I wasn't good at doing either one.

I knew that Coach didn't like me, and I sure didn't have good thoughts about him. It was hard on me when I went to confession, because I would have to confess hating Coach to the same priest each time I entered the confessional.

Because I kept my nose clean and had a study hall at the right time, twice a week I was allowed to be a crossing guard for the kindergarten classes.

The morning kindergarten class would get out around 11:30 and the afternoon class would get there about fifteen minutes later. It was my job to make sure that the little ones got safely across the street in front of the school.

When I had the duty, I'd go from study hall right to the

safety guard locker, put on a white belt that had a strap that went over one shoulder, walk down the sidewalk to Route 5 to the crosswalk, and wait for the little ones either to come out of school or down the sidewalk on the other side of the street headed toward school.

When they got close to the road, I'd tell them to wait, check for traffic, go to the center of the street, hold up my hand to stop any traffic, and wave the students across.

I took my job very seriously and never had a little one end up under the wheels of a car or truck.

If there weren't any students around, I'd stand by the edge of the road and wait for a big truck to come by. As the truck got close to me, I'd pump my fist up and down. Once in a while the driver would sound his air horn.

I liked the job because it gave me a chance to be outside for a while. It also gave me a small feeling of power to be able to stop grownups in cars or big trucks.

Things at home followed the now usual pattern. Dad was still working at O'Hara's Meat Market in Weedsport, Terry was still mad about horses, Pat still hadn't done much wrong but missed Mary Kay, John was still short and skinny, Chris still ran around like a madman, Peg was still fun to play with, Maureen was still a normal baby but never stopped talking, and I still stayed out of Grandma Simpson's way.

Mr. Seguin

I was grateful that fall when the mowing season ended. I was really tired of it. The extra work had put a big dent in the size of my belly.

Dad showed me how to clean up the Reo mower and change

the oil to get it set for the winter. The blades needed sharpening, so we put the mower into the trunk of the car and took it to Mr. Seguin's garage on Jordan Road to have them done. Going there always fascinated me.

Mr. Seguin and his garage were unusual. He was a short man with a very raspy voice. His hands and face were always smeared with grease, and his coveralls were never clean. He'd stop working on a car when we'd walk in, wipe his hands, look at them to see if they were okay, and begin talking to us. His hands wouldn't pass Mom's inspection, but he thought they were fine.

If he were in the grease pit, Dad and I would squat down to talk to him.

Once in a while he'd say, "John, grab that big wrench and a hammer on the bench. This bolt is giving me one %^** of a time."

He'd start to pound away and swear at the same time. The swearing always helped because whatever was rusted tight would come loose.

It was a good thing that he was small, because he would have to squeeze through the narrow opening between the car and the pit to get out.

He and Dad were good friends and would always talk about things before Dad told him what he needed fixing.

His garage was made out of logs. The bark was never peeled off them when it was put up, so every time we went, there'd be more rotted bark on the ground. The inside was poorly lit and a layer of grease covered the entire floor. His cash register keys were all covered to the point that all the numbers, words and letters had disappeared. There was a small display case with candy and other types of snacks in it. Even the wrappers looked a bit dirty.

In the colder weather, Mr. Seguin would fire up the wood

stove. He had to be very careful opening and closing the stove door, because any hot coal would have put the whole garage into flames in seconds. The stove only took the chill off the place, but Mr. Seguin was used to being cold. I don't think his grease pit ever got any warmer than a mild January day.

He was one tough man. I liked him.

Mom Takes Us for a Drive

On a Saturday afternoon, Mom loaded us all into the car. Mom had the car because Dad had gotten a ride into the meat market with Mr. Bishop, who also worked there on Saturdays.

I said a short prayer before she started to back out of the driveway.

I no longer had to pray all the time when Mom drove, but I hadn't stopped praying completely because Mom had a lead foot. She'd zip from place to place like she zipped around the house and yard. If she slowed down to a normal, human speed, I'd start to worry.

We were in Weedsport in no time. We pulled up in front of Mr. O'Hara's Meat Market and unloaded.

Mr. O'Hara warmly greeted Mom. We watched Dad cutting up some meat for a customer. He had a white apron on and carved the meat quickly and with skill.

The whole store was humming with activity. Saturday was the day of the week that many customers came to buy meat for the big Sunday meal.

The raw meat didn't smell very good, but the slabs of steaks and chops sure looked great.

Mom talked to Dad while he finished cutting up a big hunk of beef into thick steaks. When he was done, he wiped his hands before Mom gave him a bag of something he had forgotten to take to work with him.

We didn't have a chance to say much to Dad because he was very busy.

I think we went there mainly because Mom didn't often get the car on Saturday and she wanted to use it on the day it wasn't around for her to drive.

Many times during the week after Dad got home, she'd take at least one of us with her to run an errand or two. She liked having the freedom.

Report Cards

The school year went by quickly. I did well in every course except English. I was still a slow reader and had some trouble understanding what I was reading.

Mom and Dad were happy with my report card and John's, very happy with Terry's, and delighted with Pat's.

Pat could do no wrong, but I never got jealous of her because she never rubbed my nose into her much-better-grades. Pat was just being Pat.

Moving to O'Neill Road

Soon after school got out, Mom and Dad gathered us all together and told us we were moving out of Stump City and into a big farmhouse in the country. For years I had dreamed about living in a bigger house. Now that it was going to happen, I was torn between leaving and staying.

I had made good friends, and didn't want to leave them

behind. I also didn't want to start all over again making friends in a new school.

The folks loaded us all into the 57 Chevy, and we went to see the house. It was only five miles or so away.

When we saw the size of the house, we were all happy. It was huge. I also noticed the size of the lawn. It was beyond huge. I figured it would take at least two hours to mow.

We went into the house and ran from room to room in awe. There were four bedrooms upstairs with a huge bathroom. The downstairs had a kitchen in a newer section of the house and four large rooms. It was more than two times bigger than our old house. We were all finally getting some elbow room.

Just Don't Drink the Water

We spent lots of time cleaning, painting, and fixing up the old farmhouse before we moved in. It was hot, so we all drank lots of water.

We all got sick, and I got the sickest.

For several days, I was doubled over in pure agony, had a temperature, and couldn't keep anything in my system. The rest of the family was sick, but felt better after a day or two.

Dad asked Mr. Powers, the man who was selling us the house, about the water because it had an off-taste. Mr. Powers forgot to tell Dad not to drink from any faucet except the kitchen one because the rest of the faucets only had cistern water coming out of them. He was very upset that he hadn't told Dad.

Dad checked the cistern to see how it looked. He wouldn't tell us.

I was a good four inches taller than Mom now and knew I

could see over the edge of the cistern, so when I was well enough to go back up to the new house again, I looked down into it with a flashlight. It was a mistake to use the light.

Ignorance would have been very bliss!

I won't tell you what was floating in it, but it's a wonder that none of us hadn't died.

I had all kinds of emotions running through my mind in a jumbled way. They all circled around how we were pulling up roots from the only home I ever knew, moving away from people who were like extended family, and going to a new school.

A thought hit me like a hammer. We were close to Skaneateles! Didn't Mary Cotter go to school there?

Dad borrowed a big farm truck from Mr. Powers to move all of our belongings into the new house on O'Neill Road.

I was plenty big and strong enough to help Dad. By early afternoon, we had made three trips and headed back for the last load.

After we loaded the remainder of our meager well-worn possessions, I watched as Dad took out the old house key. He closed the door with care, locked it, looked at the key and rubbed it with his bad thumb.

Dad slowly put the key in his pocket as we went down the sidewalk to the truck.

For some reason, we both turned at the same time to look at the house.

Neither one of us said a word. I know I couldn't, and I don't think Dad could either.

Dad drove slowly up our dead end road with no name, made a right turn onto Stump Road, and continued to drive slowly up the road. He slowed down a little more as we passed his old homestead.

Thoughts of days gone by were flowing through my head as

we took a left onto County Line Road and drove out of Stump City.

I kept looking out the side window as we went up the hill and forced myself not to look back. I had tears in my eyes, and I didn't want Dad to see them.

Did Dad have tears in his eyes?

I'll never know because I didn't stop looking out the side window until the tears were about dry in my eyes.

Life would never be the same again, and I knew it—just like I now knew the real truth about the five-day vacations.

THE END

739755

Made in the USA